MODERN CROCHETED SHAWLS & WRAPS

MODERN CROCHETED SHAWLS & WRAPS

35 STYLISH WAYS TO KEEP WARM FROM LACY SHAWLS TO CHUNKY WRAPS

LAURA STRUTT

Dedicated to Charlotte Styles and Hazel Cruickshank, my Granny and Grandma, for filling my childhood with knitting, crochet and all kinds of crafts, even though I probably didn't pay as much attention as I should have!

Published in 2016 by CICO Books
An imprint of Ryland Peters & Small Ltd
20–21 Jockey's Fields
London WC1R 4BW
341 E 116th St
New York, NY 10029

www.rylandpeters.com

10 9 8 7 6 5 4 3

A CIP catalog record for this book is available from the Library of Congress and the British Library.

ISBN: 978-1-78249-311-2

Printed in China

Editor: Rachel Atkinson
Pattern checker: Jemima Bicknell
Designer: Geoff Borin
Photographer: Emma Mitchell and Penny Wincer
Stylist: Nel Haynes

Art director: Sally Powell
Head of production: Patricia Harrington
Publishing manager: Penny Craig
Publisher: Cindy Richards

CONTENTS

INTRODUCTION

A crochet shawl is a colourful way to liven up your wardrobe: from classic triangle shawls, rectangular wraps and capes, to cowls and cover-ups, there is something for every style and season. Not only can these stylish pieces complete your look in an instant, there is often nothing quite as comforting as wrapping oneself up in a sumptuous hand-crocheted wrap – and the larger ones can double up as throws, to be draped over sofas or beds.

Crochet is one of my favourite creative pastimes. With its wide variety of stitches, techniques and creative possibilities, it is both a relaxing and calming pursuit and a challenging yet hugely rewarding craft. There is also great satisfaction to be had from creating your own garments to wear, and shawls can be worn by all of us, regardless of body shape, size, age, gender or personal style. What I love most about shawls is that these clever accessories can really transform a look and the classic shapes and structure give so many options for colours, stitch patterns, techniques and even construction, to create a unique wearable piece. When I created this collection of 35 modern crochet shawl designs I wanted to offer something for everyone, from cosy capes such as On the Moors, and chunky makes like the Archer's Cowl, to feminine cover-ups and clever constructions as seen in Rose Garden and Eternally Green.

Crocheted shawls and wraps are a fabulous way to try out new techniques, like making yo-yos for the Yo-yo Throw, or granny hexagons for piecing together a Pansies and Fuchsias geometric throw. As well as being able to try a wealth of techniques and stitch designs when creating your shawl, you can also have lots of fun with colour: try creating ombré effects as used for Soft Summer Night, make a statement with colour blocks for Navajo Sunrise or even raid your stash for the mix-and-match design of Stash-buster Stripes. The possibilities are endless!

I hope that this modern collection of crochet shawls will win its way into your heart as you fill your wardrobe and your home with wonderful handmade creations!

Happy Crocheting!

BEFORE YOU BEGIN

Crochet shawls, wraps and throws are very satisfying projects to make – not only are you able to try out a range of different techniques and stitch patterns, but you also create a unique handmade accessory to wear with pride!

The projects in this book are great as statement accessories or cosy cover-ups, or simply for a flash of pick-me-up colour! What's more, because these are all "one size" makes, they are ideal for any body shape, size, gender or age and also make ideal and thoughtful gifts for friends and family.

TIPS AND HINTS

- Many of the patterns use multiple shades of yarns, in repeated motifs like the Pansies and Fuchsias geometric throw (page 18) or stripes like the Stash-buster Stripes (page 12). Colour changes will leave lots of yarn ends to weave in, which can be very time consuming, so try to weave in the ends as you work to make the process of finishing your project quicker and easier.

- Locking stitch markers make a great addition to your crochet tool kit and are used in a number of projects featured throughout this book including Paintbox Palette (page 34) and Navajo Sunrise (page 28). Placing a marker in a key stitch, such as the central "spine" of a shawl, or increase and shaping points, will help you to keep track of where you are in a row, or you can use them to indicate where buttons should be stitched. Remember to move the stitch marker up with each row or use two in tandem with one another. Safety pins can be used at a pinch, but mind they don't snag or leave rust marks on your crochet fabric.

- Crochet shawls benefit hugely from blocking once complete; not only does blocking help the pieces to lay neatly and to the given measurements, it also opens up the stitches to really show off the pretty details of your hard work and gives a professional finish. You can block your finished make either with steam from the iron, or by soaking in lukewarm water and pinning into shape to dry. Remember to check the ball band of the yarn for specific details on washing the yarn, and take care when steaming acrylic and acrylic blend yarns as they can easily stretch out of shape – wet blocking will be a much better option. Cotton and silk yarns can be blocked firmly to encourage the fibres to sit neatly in place.

- Some of the projects in this book are quite large, for example the Yo-yo Throw (page 58) and By the Lake (page 114). The scale of these makes can initially be daunting, but breaking them down into sections of different stitch pattern repeats or colours will give you smaller goals to work towards – "I'll just do one more section in yarn A" or "five more repeats of this two-row stitch pattern" and so on.

- It is very important, particularly for the larger single-colour projects, that you have enough yarn before starting. Buying all the required yarn in one go can be expensive but it will mean you have balls or skeins from the same dye lot. Different dye lots can vary slightly in colour and changes in dye lots partway through a project will be noticeable.

- Almost all the makes featured in this book can easily be sized up or down by working fewer or more repeats of the stitch patterns, or simply by selecting a finer or chunkier yarn and matching with the appropriate hook size. Making a project larger will of course require more yarn and it is also important to remember that triangular, granny square and inside-out circular shaped patterns grow in stitch counts as well as rows as the shape expands. Ensure you buy more yarn than you estimate so you don't run out halfway through a row. It is also worth bearing in mind that certain stitches, such as the puff stitch featured in Emerald Puff (page 38) and Pretty in Pink (page 16) require a lot of yarn.

YARN

Crochet shawls can be made from almost any style, thickness, fibre and finish of yarn. Each will have different properties and lend itself to different looks for the finished piece. Chunky and super-chunky yarns create a denser fabric and make for wonderfully quick and cosy projects, whilst projects using lighter weight yarns might take slightly longer to complete, but will create finished designs with more drape and fluidity.

The patterns in this book showcase a range of effects and finishes you can achieve by using different weights, fibres and styles of yarn – you can even raid your yarn stash to create these makes, just be sure to check the details of the yarn weights, amounts and tension when substituting yarn.

A guide for the tension is given with each pattern, and whilst matching this given tension is not as paramount when making shawls as with more fitted garments, it is important to achieve a tension as close as possible to the one provided so your finished make has the same look, feel and sizing as shown in the photographs. Check your tension before starting the project and make adjustments by simply switching the size of the hook – if your tension is too tight and the stitches on your tension swatch are smaller than those recommended, try using a hook one size larger. Similarly, if your stitches are too large, switch to a hook one size smaller and rework the tension swatch. See page 120 for information on tension swatches.

Maintaining an even tension throughout your project is important for a neat and tidy finish as all the stitches will be of a similar size. This is particularly important for projects with feature stitches such as the puff stitch in Stash-buster Stripes (page 12) where even tension will create a series of uniform puff stitches throughout the shawl.

If you are working on a larger, more involved shawl such as Splash of Orange (page 96) and you want to take a break from it, be sure to make a note of the hook you have been using so that when you return to it you will be able to achieve the same, consistent tension.

EQUIPMENT

Crochet hooks: The patterns in this book indicate the size of hook to use with the yarn listed for the project. You can adjust these where necessary to accommodate yarn substitutions and to adjust your tension. How you hold your hook is a matter of preference – left-handed or right-handed, some like to hold their hook in a pencil-grip, while others prefer to hold it in their fist. There is no right or wrong way, as long as you are able to move your wrist freely and can comfortably work neat and even stitches. See page 118 in the techniques section for further guidance.

Crochet hooks used in the book:

UK/Metric	US
4mm	G/6
5mm	H/8
6mm	J/10
8mm	L/11
9mm	M/13
15 or 16mm	P/16

Tapestry and yarn needles: These are used to secure the ends of the yarn at the start and end of the project and also where changing colours. For heavier weight yarns, try using a split-eye needle or even a small crochet hook to secure in the ends neatly.

Sewing needle and thread: Handy to have for securing buttons and fastenings to finished makes.

Tape measure: Always useful for checking tension swatches and finished sizes when blocking.

Rust-proof pins: For holding your project in shape while it is being blocked.

ABBREVIATIONS

cm	Centimetre(s)
ch	Chain
ch-sp(s)	Chain-space(s)
dc	Double crochet
dc2tog	Double crochet 2 stitches together
dtr	Double treble crochet
FLO	Front loop only
FPtr	Front post treble crochet
g	Gram(mes)
htr	Half treble crochet
in	Inch(es)
m	Metre(s)
mm	Millimetre(s)
oz	Ounce(s)
PS	Puff stitch
rep(s)	Repeat(s)
RS	Right side of work
sl	Slip
st(s)	Stitch(es)
t-ch	Turning chain
tr	Treble crochet
tr2tog	Treble crochet 2 stitches together
yd(s)	Yard(s)
yrh	Yarn round hook
WS	Wrong side of work

SKILL LEVEL

Each project includes a star rating as a skill level guide and you will find the project includes the techniques listed below:

★☆☆ Projects for first-time crocheters using basic stitches with minimal shaping.

★★☆ Projects using basic stitches, repetitive stitch patterns, simple colour changes, and simple shaping and finishing.

★★★ Projects using a variety of techniques, such as basic lace patterns or colour patterns, mid-level shaping and finishing.

Chapter 1

BRIGHT AND BEAUTIFUL

Skill Rating: ★★☆

Stash-buster STRIPES

Create your own sampler shawl by using a variety of colours and a range of different stitches. This super-sized, top down design makes a fantastic statement piece for your wardrobe.

MATERIALS

- Cascade 220 (100% Peruvian Highland wool; 200m/220yds per 100g/3½oz skein) aran-weight yarn

  3 x 100g (3½oz) skeins in shade 8011 Aspen Heather (A)

  1 x 100g (3½oz) skein in shade 8907 Caribbean (B)

  1 x 100g (3½oz) skein in shade 9463B Gold (C)

  1 x 100g (3½oz) skein in shade 8911 Grape Jelly (D)

  1 x 100g (3½oz) skein in shade 7801 Rouge Red (E)

  1 x 100g (3½oz) skein in shade 8311 Mineral Blue (F)
- 5mm (US H/8) crochet hook
- Locking stitch marker
- Tapestry needle

FINISHED MEASUREMENTS

90cm (35½in) deep x 212cm (83½in) wide

TENSION

14 sts and 8 rows to measure 10cm (4in)

ABBREVIATIONS

See page 9.

SPECIAL STITCHES

Puff Stitch (PS): *Yarn round hook, pass through stitch, draw yarn through, keeping the yarn loops long; rep from * a further 5 times, yarn round hook again and draw through all loops on the hook, work 1ch to close the stitch.

FOR THE SHAWL

Foundation: Using yarn A and 5mm (US H/8) hook, make a magic ring. Work 4ch (counts as 1tr and 1ch), *1tr, 1ch into ring; rep from * twice more, 1tr into ring. Draw up tightly to conceal the hole and create a small half-moon shape with 5 sts. Turn and continue in rows as follows:

Row 1: 4ch (counts as 1tr and 1ch throughout), 1tr in same st, 1tr in ch-sp, 1tr in next st, 1tr in ch-sp, 1ch, 1tr and place marker in the st to indicate centre spine, 1ch, 1tr in ch-sp, 1tr in next st, 1tr in ch-sp, [1tr, 1ch, 1tr] in last st (third ch of 4ch from previous row), turn. (11 sts)

Row 2: 4ch, 1tr in same st, 1tr in ch-sp, 1tr in each of next 4 sts, 1tr in ch-sp, 1ch, 1tr in marked st, move marker, 1ch, 1tr in ch-sp, 1tr in each of next 4 sts, 1tr in ch-sp, [1tr, 1ch, 1tr] in last st, turn. (17 sts)

Row 3: 4ch, 1tr in same st, 1tr in ch-sp, 1tr in each of next 7 sts, 1tr in ch-sp, 1ch, 1tr in marked st, move marker, 1ch, 1tr in ch-sp, 1tr in each of next 7 sts, 1tr in ch-sp, [1tr, 1ch, 1tr] in last st, turn. (23 sts)

Tip

Use a locking stitch marker to keep track of the central "spine" stitch of this shawl by placing it in the 1tr as indicated in the pattern and move it up with each row as you work.

Row 4: 4ch, 1tr in same st, 1tr in ch-sp, 1tr in each of next 10 sts, 1tr in ch-sp, 1ch, 1tr in marked st, move marker, 1ch, 1tr in ch-sp, 1tr in each of next 10 sts, 1tr in ch-sp, [1tr, 1ch, 1tr] in last st, turn. (29 sts)

Row 5: 4ch, 1tr in same st, 1tr in ch-sp, 1tr in each st to marked st, 1tr in ch-sp, 1ch, 1tr in marked st, move marker, 1ch, 1tr in ch-sp, 1tr in each st to last st, 1tr in ch-sp, [1tr, 1ch, 1tr] in last st, turn. (35 sts)

Rows 6–34: Continue in pattern, working reps of Row 5 for a further 28 rows and increasing 6tr with each row (3tr in each half of shawl) as set. (33 rows worked in total – 203 sts)

Row 35: Change to yarn B, 4ch, 1tr in same st, 1tr in ch-sp, *miss 1 st, 1ch, 1tr in next st; rep from * to marked st, 1tr in ch-sp, 1ch, 1tr in marked st, move marker, 1ch, 1tr in ch-sp, **1tr in next st, miss 1 st, 1ch; rep from ** to last ch-sp, 1tr in ch-sp, [1tr, 1ch, 1tr] in last st, turn.

Row 36: Change to yarn A, 4ch, 1tr in same st, 1tr in ch-sp, 1tr in each st and ch-sp to marked st, 1ch, 1tr in marked st, move marker, 1ch, 1tr in each st and ch-sp to last ch-sp, 1tr in last ch-sp, [1tr, 1ch, 1tr] in last st, turn.

Row 37: Change to yarn C, work as Row 35.

Row 38: Change to yarn A, work as Row 36.

Row 39: Change to yarn D, work as Row 35.

Row 40: Change to yarn A, work as Row 36.

Row 41: Change to yarn E, work as Row 35.

Row 42: Change to yarn A, work as Row 36.

Row 43: Work as Row 5.

Row 44: Change to yarn B, work as Row 5.

Row 45: Change to yarn C, work as Row 5.

Row 46: Change to yarn D, work as Row 5.

Row 47: Change to yarn E, work as Row 5.

Row 48: Change to yarn B, 4ch, 1tr in same st, 1tr in ch-sp, *1PS in next st, 1ch, miss next st; rep from * to marked st, 1tr in ch-sp, 1ch, 1tr in marked st, move marker, 1ch, 1tr in ch-sp, *1ch, miss next st, 1PS in next st; rep from ** to last st, 1tr in ch-sp, [1tr, 1ch, 1tr] in last st, turn.

Row 49: Change to yarn C, 1tr in same st, 1tr in ch-sp, 1tr in each st and ch-sp to marked st, 1ch, 1tr in marked st, move marker, 1ch, 1tr in each st and ch-sp to last ch-sp, 1tr in last ch-sp, [1tr, 1ch, 1tr] in last st, turn.

Row 50: Change to yarn D, work as Row 48.

Row 51: Change to yarn E, work as Row 49.

Row 52: Change to yarn A, work as Row 35.

Row 53: Change to yarn B, work as Row 36.

Row 54: Change to yarn C, work as Row 48.

Row 55: Change to yarn D, work as Row 49.

Row 56: Change to yarn E, work as Row 48.

Row 57: Change to yarn A, work as Row 49.

Make it yours

This shawl is the perfect design for using up odd skeins of yarn in your stash, by working with a range of different colours in the lower section and even introducing your own favourite stitches to create a shawl that is unique to you.

FOR THE EDGING

The edging is worked in a continuous round along all sides of the shawl as follows:

Round 1: Change to yarn F, work 1ch (does not count as st), [1dc, 1ch, 1dc] in first st, 1dc in each st to marker, [1dc, 1ch, 1dc] in marked st, move marker, 1dc in each st to last st, [1dc, 1ch, 1dc] in last st, now continue working 2dc in each tr along upper edge, join with sl st in first st.

Round 2: *[3ch, sl st in third ch from hook (picot made), miss next st, 1dc in next st; rep from * around the entire shawl, join with a sl st in first st.

Fasten off.

MAKING UP AND FINISHING

Weave in all loose ends and block to measurements, paying close attention to the picot edging and gently pulling the points into shape.

Skill Rating: ★★★

Pretty in PINK

The voluminous puff stitches that are used to create this triangular shawl are made by looping the yarn over the hook repeatedly, resulting in a dramatic textured finish.

MATERIALS

- Caron Simply Soft (100% acrylic, 288m/315yds per 170g/6oz ball) aran-weight yarn
  5 x 170g (6oz) balls in shade 9604 Watermelon
- 5mm (US H/8) crochet hook
- Tapestry needle

FINISHED MEASUREMENTS

80cm (31½in) deep x 202cm (79½in) wide

TENSION

5.5 puff sts and 7.5 rows to measure 10cm (4in) over puff stitch

ABBREVIATIONS

See page 9.

SPECIAL STITCHES

Puff Stitch (PS): *Yarn round hook, pass through stitch, draw yarn through, keeping the yarn loops long; repeat from * a further 5 times, yarn round hook and draw through all loops on the hook, work 1ch to close the stitch.

FOR THE SHAWL

Row 1: Using 5mm (US H/8) hook, 8ch, 1PS in sixth ch from hook, 1ch, 1tr in last ch, turn. (1PS)

Row 2: 3ch (counts as 1tr throughout), 1PS in tr, 1ch, 1dc in st at top of PS on previous row, 1ch, 1PS in 3rd ch of t-ch, 1tr in same sp, turn. (2PS)

Row 3: 3ch, 1PS into tr, 1ch, 1dc in st at top of PS on previous row, 1ch, 1PS in dc on previous row, 1ch, 1dc in st at top of PS on previous row, 1ch, 1PS in 3rd ch of t-ch, 1tr in same sp, turn. (3PS)

Row 4: 3ch, 1PS into tr, *1dc in st at top of PS on previous row, 1ch, 1PS in dc on previous row, 1ch; rep from * to end working 1PS in 3rd ch of t-ch, 1tr in same sp, turn. (1PS increased)

Row 4 sets pattern.

Rows 5–65: Continue in pattern as set for a further 61 rows. (65 rows worked in total)

Tip

Puff stitch uses a large amount of yarn with each stitch. It is worth ordering slightly more than the recommended quantity to avoid running out of yarn from the same dye lot. Your supplier may accept returns of unused yarn, but if not, you will have a useful addition to your "stash."

FOR THE BORDER

Work 1ch, 1dc in each st around entire shawl working [1dc, 1ch, 1dc] in each point. Join with sl st in first st. Fasten off.

MAKING UP AND FINISHING

Weave in all loose ends and block to measurements.

Make it yours

The texture of this stitch makes a really bold shawl! Add a flash of colour with stripes by alternating yarn colours every few rows or introducing occasional pops of colour.

Skill Rating: ★★☆

Pansies and FUCHSIAS

This modular design is great for working when you are on the go, as each of the crochet hexagons is made separately, then they are joined together to create a sumptuous and cosy wrap.

MATERIALS

- Debbie Bliss Cashmerino Aran (55% wool/ 33% acrylic/12% cashmere; 90m/98yds per 50g/1¾oz ball) aran-weight yarn
  7 x 50g (1¾oz) balls in shade 027 Stone (A)
  5 x 50g (1¾oz) balls in shade 060 Fuchsia (B)
  5 x 50g (1¾oz) balls in shade 061 Jade (C)
  5 x 50g (1¾oz) balls in shade 062 Kingfisher (D)
- 5mm (US H/8) crochet hook
- Tapestry needle

FINISHED MEASUREMENTS

58cm (23in) wide x 254cm (100in) long

TENSION

1 hexagon to measure 12.5cm (5in) across

ABBREVIATIONS

See page 9.

FOR THE HEXIS

Foundation: Using yarn A and 5mm (US H/8) hook, make a magic ring. Into the ring work 3ch (counts as 1tr throughout), 2tr, 3ch, [3tr, 3ch] 5 times, join with a sl st in third ch of 3ch. Draw up tightly to conceal the hole. (18 sts and 6 ch-sp)

Round 1: Change to yarn B. 4ch (counts as 1tr and 1ch), *[3tr, 3ch, 3tr] in next 3ch-sp, 1ch; rep from * to last ch-sp, [3tr, 3ch, 2tr] in last ch-sp, join with a sl st in third ch of 4ch.

Round 2: Change to yarn C. 3ch (counts as 1tr), 2tr in first ch-sp, 1ch, *[2tr, 1ch, 2tr] in next ch-sp, 1ch, 3tr in next ch-sp, 1ch; rep from * to last ch-sp, [2tr, 1ch, 2tr] in last ch-sp, join with a sl st in third ch of 3ch. Fasten off.

Weave in ends to save having to do them all at the end.

Make 95 hexis in a range of colour combinations using yarn A for the centre and yarns B, C and D for the outer sections and include a few single coloured hexis too.

Weave in any remaining ends and block the hexis to size.

Tip

Block the hexagons before joining – this will help to match them up and give a neat finish to the blanket.

Lay out the hexis in a random pattern with the following number in each row:

Row 1: 1.

Row 2: 2.

Row 3: 3.

Row 4: 4.

Rows 5–18: 5.

Row 19: 4.

Row 20: 3.

Row 21: 2.

Row 22: 1.

FOR THE WRAP

Using yarn A and 5mm (US H/8) hook, join the hexis using the following "join as you go" method:

Begin by working 1dc in each st around a hexi to create a border working [1dc, 1ch, 1dc] in each corner st. Align second motif at corner for join, work [1dc, 1ch, 1dc] in corner of second motif, take the loop off the hook, pass the hook front to back through the corresponding stitch on the first motif and draw through as a sl st, work 1dc in next st on second motif. Rep along side of second motif, taking the loop off the hook after each st and taking it though the other motif as a sl st to join before working next st; continue in this way till the side is joined. Continue working 1dc in each st around remaining sides of the hexi. Join next hexi in same manner and continue until all of the blocks are joined in.

MAKING UP AND FINISHING

Weave in any loose ends and gently block to final measurements.

Make it yours

This design is made with a random placement of crochet hexagons. For a more uniform look, work in a striped repeat pattern of coloured motifs.

This pattern would look amazing in ombré shades of the same colour.

Skill Rating: ★★☆

Boho CHIC

These striking chevrons are worked to create a neat overlapping and layered effect, which plays on the contrast between the bright and bold colours. The chevrons are neatly attached to a shaped, button-up yoke making it an easy garment to slip on and wear.

MATERIALS

- Rowan Cotton Glace (100% cotton; 115m/126yds per 50g/1¾oz ball) DK-weight yarn
  - 2 x 50g (1¾oz) balls of shade 843 Toffee (A)
  - 2 x 50g (1¾oz) balls of shade 849 Winsor (B)
  - 2 x 50g (1¾oz) balls of shade 832 Persimmon (C)
  - 3 x 50g (1¾oz) balls of shade 725 Ecru (D)
- 4mm (US G/6) crochet hook
- 2 x 2cm (¾in) buttons
- Tapestry needle

FINISHED MEASUREMENTS

82cm (32in) wide around shoulders x 53.5cm (21in) long

TENSION

28 sts and 13 rows to measure 10cm (4in) over chevron pattern

ABBREVIATIONS

See page 9.

FOR THE CHEVRON PATTERN

Foundation: Using yarn A and 4mm (US G/6) hook, make 226ch.

** **Row 1 (RS):** 1ch (does not count as st), dc2tog, 1dc in each of next 6 ch, *3dc in next ch, 1dc in each of next 8 ch, miss 2 ch, 1dc in each of next 8 ch; rep from * to last 9 ch, 3dc in next ch, 1dc in each of next 6 ch, dc2tog.

Row 2 (WS): 1ch, dc2tog, 1dc in each of next 6 sts, *3dc in next st, 1dc in each of next 8 sts, miss 2 sts, 1dc in each of next 8 sts; rep from * to last 9 sts, 3dc in next st, 1dc in each of next 6 sts, dc2tog.

Row 2 sets pattern.

Rows 3–8: Rep Row 2.

Row 9: Rep Row 2 but work through the front loop only (FLO) of each st.

Row 10: Rep Row 2 working through both loops again.

Fasten off.

With RS of chevrons facing but working in the unworked loop of sts in the previous stripe at back of work (see Tip, below), join yarn B and rep Rows 1–10.

Note: When repeating Row 1, you will be working into stitches rather than the chain, i.e. "1dc in each of next 6 sts".

Tip

When joining in the new yarn for the next chevron in the colour sequence, keep the work with the right side facing you and fold the work over to expose the unworked back loops on Row 9 of the previous chevron strip.

universal

With RS of chevrons facing but working in the unworked loop of sts in the previous stripe at back of work (see Tip, page 22), join yarn C and rep Rows 1–10.

With RS of chevrons facing but working in the unworked loop of sts in the previous stripe at back of work (see Tip, page 22), join yarn D and rep Rows 1–4, followed by Row 9 and then work Row 10.

Rep from ** once more to create a second set of chevrons.

Fasten off.

FOR THE YOKE

Row 1: With RS facing and using 4mm (US G/6) hook, re-join yarn D at the top point of the first chevron.*12ch, 1dc in next chevron point; rep from * to end, turn.

Row 2: 1ch, 1dc in each ch and st to end, turn. (156 sts)

Rows 3–4: 1ch, 1dc in each st to end, turn.

Row 5: 3ch (counts as 1tr throughout), 1tr in each st to end.

Row 6: 3ch, 1tr in each of next 22 sts, tr2tog, 1tr, tr2tog, 1tr in each of next 21 sts, tr2tog, 1tr, tr2tog, 1 tr in each of next 47 sts, tr2tog, 1tr, tr2tog, 1tr in each of next 21 sts, tr2tog, 1tr, tr2tog, 1tr in each st to end, turn. (148 sts)

Row 7: 3ch, 1tr in each of next 19 sts, [tr2tog] twice, 1tr, [tr2tog] twice, 1tr in each of next 15 sts, [tr2tog] twice, 1tr, [tr2tog] twice, 1tr in each of next 41 sts, [tr2tog] twice, 1tr, [tr2tog] twice, 1tr in each of next 15 sts, [tr2tog] twice, 1tr, [tr2tog] twice, 1tr in each st to end, turn. (132 sts)

Row 8: 3ch, 1tr in each of next 18 sts, [tr2tog] twice, 1tr, [tr2tog] twice, 1tr in each of next 11 sts, [tr2tog] twice, 1tr, [tr2tog] twice, 1tr in each of next 37 sts, [tr2tog] twice, 1tr, [tr2tog] twice, 1tr in each of next 11 sts, [tr2tog] twice, 1tr, [tr2tog] twice, 1tr in each st to end. (116 sts)

Row 9: 3ch, 1tr in next each of 15 sts, [tr2tog] twice, 1tr, [tr2tog] twice, 1tr in each of next 7 sts, [tr2tog] twice, 1tr, [tr2tog] twice, 1tr in each of next 33 sts, [tr2tog] twice, 1tr, [tr2tog] twice, 1tr in each of next 7 sts, [tr2tog] twice, 1tr, [tr2tog] twice, 1tr in each st to end. (100 sts)

Row 10: 3ch, 1tr in each of next 13 sts, [tr2tog] twice, 1tr, [tr2tog] twice, 1tr in each of next 3 sts, [tr2tog] twice, 1tr, [tr2tog] twice, 1tr in each of next 29 sts, [tr2tog] twice, 1tr, [tr2tog] twice, 1tr in each of next 3 sts, [tr2tog] twice, 1tr, [tr2tog] twice, 1tr in each st to end. (84 sts)

Rows 11–12: 1ch, 1dc in each st to end, turn.

Fasten off.

FOR THE FRONT EDGE

With RS facing and using 4mm (US G/6) hook, re-join yarn D at the bottom of the chevron strip and work 1ch, 1dc in each st up the side to the top of the yoke. Fasten off.

Rep to add a dc border to the second side of the cloak and at the centre front point of the yoke, work 12ch and join with a sl st in first st to create buttonhole loop, then work 12dc into loop and fasten off.

MAKING UP AND FINISHING

Weave in all loose ends and block to measurements.

Position button to align with buttonhole loop on corresponding side of yoke and sew securely in place. Stitch on a second button on the opposite side of the yoke for a decorative finish.

Make it yours

The chevron section can be extended to make a longer cloak design; simply continue in the chevron pattern as set to the desired size and adjust the yarn quantities accordingly.

Skill Rating: ★★☆

Seashore STRIPES

Cotton yarns make great summer garments. This light, bright shawl features a range of complementary shades worked into a repeated stripe pattern, and perfect for a cover-up on chilly summer evenings.

FOR THE SHAWL

Foundation: Using yarn A and 4mm (US G/6) hook, make a magic ring. Work 4ch (counts as 1tr and 1ch), *1tr, 1ch into ring; rep from * twice more, 1tr into ring. Draw up tightly to conceal the hole and create a small half-moon shape with 5 sts. Turn and continue in rows as follows:

Row 1: 4ch (counts as 1tr and 1ch throughout), 1tr in same st, 1tr in ch-sp, 1tr in next st, 1tr in ch-sp, 1ch, 1tr in next st and place marker in the st to indicate centre spine, 1ch, 1tr in ch-sp, 1tr in next st, 1tr in ch-sp, [1tr, 1ch, 1tr] in last st (third ch of 4ch from previous row), turn. (11 sts and 4 ch-sp)

Row 2: 4ch, 1tr in same st, 1tr in ch-sp, 1tr in each of next 4 sts, 1tr in ch-sp, 1ch, 1tr in marked st, move marker, 1ch, 1tr in ch-sp, 1tr in each of next 4 sts, 1tr in ch-sp, [1tr, 1ch, 1tr] in last st, turn.

Row 3: 4ch, 1tr in same st, 1tr in ch-sp, 1tr in each st to ch-sp before marked st, 1tr in ch-sp, 1ch, 1tr in marked st, move marker, 1ch, 1tr in ch-sp, 1tr in each st to last ch-sp, 1tr in ch-sp, [1tr, 1ch, 1tr] in last st, turn.

Row 3 sets pattern.

Tip

Use a locking stitch marker to keep track of the central "spine" stitch of this shawl by placing it in the 1tr as indicated in the pattern and moving it up with each row as you work.

MATERIALS

- Rowan Cotton Glace (100% cotton; 115m/126yds per 50g/1¾oz ball) DK-weight yarn
  - 5 x 50g (1¾oz) balls in shade 730 Oyster (A)
  - 1 x 50g (1¾oz) ball in shade 832 Persimmon (B)
  - 1 x 50g (1¾oz) ball in shade 749 Sky (C)
  - 2 x 50g (1¾oz) balls in shade 856 Mineral (D)
- 4mm (US G/6) crochet hook
- Locking stitch marker
- Tapestry needle

FINISHED MEASUREMENTS

76.5cm (30in) deep x 183cm (72in) wide

TENSION

15tr and 9 rows to measure 10cm (4in) after blocking

ABBREVIATIONS

See page 9.

Make it yours

This striped design can be created with any of your favourite colours; pick three shades and a neutral tone for yarn A to create the most dramatic effect.

Continue in pattern as set for a further 50 rows (53 rows in total), changing colours in the following order:

Rows 4–5: Yarn B.

Rows 6–9: Yarn A.

Rows 10–11: Yarn C.

Rows 12–15: Yarn A.

Rows 16–17: Yarn D.

Rows 18–21: Yarn A.

Rows 22–23: Yarn B.

Rows 24–27: Yarn A.

Rows 28–29: Yarn C.

Rows 30–33: Yarn A.

Rows 34–35: Yarn D.

Rows 36–39: Yarn A.

Rows 40–41: Yarn B.

Rows 42–45: Yarn A.

Rows 46–47: Yarn C.

Rows 48–51: Yarn A.

Rows 52–53: Yarn D.

Do not fasten off.

FOR THE BORDER

Row 1: Change to yarn A, 1ch, 2dc in first st, 1dc in each st to marked st, [1dc, 1ch, 1dc] in marked st, move marker, 1dc in each st to last st, 2dc in last st, turn.

Row 2: Rep Row 1.

Row 3: Change to yarn B and rep Row 1. Fasten off.

MAKING UP AND FINISHING

Weave in all loose ends and block to measurements.

Skill Rating: ★☆☆

Navajo SUNRISE

Crocheted from the top down, the simple structure of this shawl makes a fabulous canvas for playing with colour. Add a bright pop of your favourite shade to create this colour block design.

PATTERN NOTES

Use a locking stitch marker to keep track of the central "spine" stitch of this shawl by placing it in the second of the 3dc or 3tr at the centre of the row as indicated in the pattern and move it up with each row as you work.

FOR THE SHAWL

Foundation: Using yarn A and 4mm (US G/6) hook, make 6ch.

Row 1: 2dc in second ch from hook, 1dc in next ch, 3dc in next ch (this sets centre spine), 1dc in next ch, 2dc in last ch, turn. (9 sts)

Row 2: 1ch (does not count as st throughout), 2dc in first st, 1dc in each of next 3 sts, 3dc in next st and place marker in second of 3dc to indicate centre spine st, 1dc in each of next 3 sts, 2dc in last st, turn. (13 sts)

Row 3: 1ch, 2dc in first st, 1dc in each st to marked centre spine st, 3dc in spine st and move marker, 1dc in each st to last st, 2dc in last st, turn. (17 sts)

Row 4: Rep Row 3. (21 sts)

Row 5: Rep Row 3. (25 sts)

Row 6 (Eyelet row): 3ch (counts as 1tr), 1tr in same st, *1ch, miss 1 st, 1tr in next st; rep from * to 1 st before marked centre spine st, 1ch, miss 1 st, 3tr in centre spine st and move marker, **1ch, miss 1 st, 1tr in next st; rep from ** to last 2 st, 1ch, miss 1 st, 2tr in last st. (17 sts and 12 ch-sps)

MATERIALS

- Sublime Extra Fine Merino DK (100% extra fine merino wool; 116m/127yds per 50g/1¾oz ball) DK-weight yarn
  5 x 50g (1¾oz) balls in shade 361 Gem (A)
  2 x 50g (1¾oz) balls in shade 373 Pumpkin (B)
- 4mm (US G/6) crochet hook
- Locking stitch marker
- Tapestry needle

FINISHED MEASUREMENTS

61cm (24in) deep x 128cm (50½in) wide

TENSION

22 sts and 20 rows to measure 10cm (4in)

ABBREVIATIONS

See page 9.

Tip

The double crochet stitch creates a dense fabric. Take time to firmly block the finished shawl to open up and relax the stitches before wearing. See page 125 for tips on blocking.

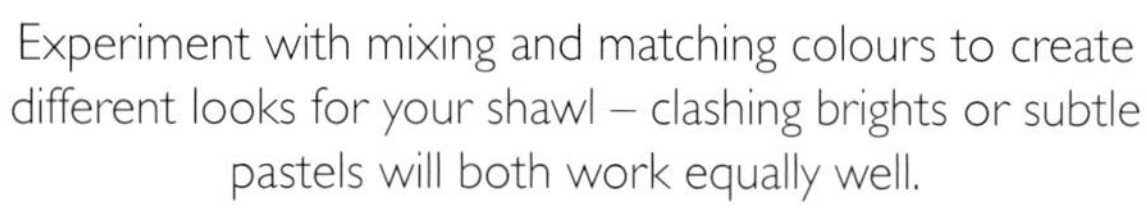

Make it yours

Experiment with mixing and matching colours to create different looks for your shawl – clashing brights or subtle pastels will both work equally well.

Row 7: 1ch, 2dc in first st, 1dc in each st and ch-sp to marked centre spine st, 3dc in spine st and move marker, 1dc in each st and ch-sp to last st, 2dc in last st, turn.

Rows 8–11: 1ch, 2dc in first st, 1dc in each st to marked centre spine st, 3dc in spine st and move marker, 1dc in each st to last st, 2dc in last st, turn.

Row 12 (Eyelet row): 3ch (counts as 1tr), 1tr in same st, *1ch, miss 1 st, 1tr in next st; rep from * to 1 st before centre st, 1ch, miss 1 st, 3tr in spine st and move marker, **1ch, miss 1 st, 1tr in next st; rep from ** to last 2 st, 1ch, miss 1 st, 2tr in last st.

Rows 7–12 set pattern.

Rows 13–65: Continue in pattern as set, repeating rows 7-12 until 65 rows have been worked in total, ending with Row 11. (265 sts)

Row 66 (Eyelet row): Change to yarn B and rep Row 12. (137 sts and 132 ch-sps)

Row 67: Change to yarn A, 1ch, 2dc in first st, 1dc in each st and ch-sp to marked centre spine st, 3dc in spine st and move marker, 1dc in each st and ch-sp to last st, 2dc in last st, turn.

Rows 68–71: Work in pattern as set. (289 sts)

Row 72 (Eyelet row): Change to yarn B and rep Row 12. (149 sts and 144 ch-sps)

Continue in yarn B.

Rows 73–77: Continue in pattern as set. (313 sts)

Row 78 (Eyelet row): Rep Row 12. (161 sts and 156 ch-sps)

Row 79: Change to yarn A, 1ch, 2dc in first st, 1dc in each st and ch-sp to marked centre spine st, 3dc in centre spine st and move marker, 1dc in each st and ch-sp to last st, 2dc in last st, turn. (321 sts)

Row 80 (Eyelet row): Change to yarn B, rep Row 12. (165 sts and 160 ch-sps)

Row 81: Change to yarn A, 1dc in each st, [1dc, 1ch, 1dc] in spine st and remove marker, 1dc in each st to end.

Fasten off.

MAKING UP AND FINISHING

Weave in all loose ends and block firmly to measurements.

Note that the fabric is quite dense so you may find the finished shawl springs back on itself slightly once dry.

Skill Rating: ★★☆

Flower GARDEN

This fabulously feminine wrap features neat little flowers on a lattice style background. The flowers are created across two rows, with half the flower worked on each, so it doesn't take long before you can see the design taking shape.

MATERIALS

- Caron Simply Soft Paints (100% acrylic; 190m/208yds per 113g/4oz ball) aran-weight yarn
  6 x 113g (4oz) balls in shade 0016 Rainbow Bright
- 5mm (US H/8) crochet hook
- Tapestry needle

FINISHED MEASUREMENTS

63.5cm (25in) wide x 203cm (80in) long

TENSION

1 flower to measure 4cm (1½in)

ABBREVIATIONS

See page 9.

FOR THE WRAP

Row 1: Using the 5mm (US H/8) hook, make 6ch, join with sl st in first ch to make a circle and into the circle work [sl st, (3ch, 2tr, 3ch, sl st) twice] (1 half flower made), *19ch, sl st in sixth ch from hook to make a circle, into the circle work [sl st, (3ch, 2tr, 3ch, sl st) twice] (1 half flower made); rep from * a further 5 times, turn. (7 half flowers)

Row 2: Into the circle work [sl st, (3ch, 2tr, 3ch, sl st) twice] (second half of flower made), *13dc across ch, into the circle work [sl st, (3ch, 2tr, 3ch, sl st) twice] (second half of flower made); rep from * to end, turn. (7 flowers complete)

Row 3: 19ch, sl st in sixth ch from hook to make a circle, and into the circle work [sl st, 3ch, 2tr, 3ch, sl st], 1dtr in seventh dc, into the same circle work [sl st, 3ch, 2tr, 3ch, sl st] (1 half flower made), *6ch, 1dtr in sl st between petals of half flower in row below, 12ch, join with sl st in sixth ch from hook to make a circle, into the circle work [sl st, 3ch, 2tr, 3ch, sl st], 1dtr in 7th dc, into the same circle work [sl st, 3ch, 2tr, 3ch, sl st] (1 half flower made); rep from * to last flower, 6ch, 1dtr in sl st between petals of last half flower in row below, turn.

Make it yours

This design is worked in a bright and bold variegated yarn but would look equally stunning in a subtle solid shade.

Row 4: 1ch, 1dc in top of dtr, 1ch in each of next 6ch, into the circle work [sl st, (3ch, 2tr, 3ch, sl st) twice] (second half of flower made), *13dc across ch, into the circle work [sl st, (3ch, 2tr, 3ch, sl st) twice] (second half of flower made); rep from * to end, 1dc each of next 6 ch, turn.

Row 5: 12ch, sl st in sixth ch from hook to make a circle, into the circle work [sl st, (3ch, 2tr, 3ch, sl st) twice] (1 half flower made), 6ch, 1dtr in sl st between petals of half flower in row below, *12ch, join with sl st in sixth ch from hook to make a circle, into the circle work [sl st, 3ch, 2tr, 3ch, sl st] (1 half flower made), 1dtr in seventh dc, [sl st, 3ch, 2tr, 3ch, sl st] (1 half flower made), 6ch, 1dtr in sl st between petals of half flower in row below; rep from * to end, 12ch, join with sl st in sixth ch from hook to make a circle, into the circle work [sl st, 3ch, 2tr, 3ch, sl st], 1dtr in last dc, into same circle work [sl st, 3ch, 2tr, 3ch, sl st] (1 half flower made), turn.

Row 6: *Into the circle work [sl st, (3ch, 2tr, 3ch, sl st) twice] (second half of flower made), 13dc across ch; rep from * to end, turn.

Rows 3–6 set the pattern.

Continue as set working repeats of Rows 3–6 until the piece measures 203cm (80in) ending with Row 6.

Fasten off.

MAKING UP AND FINISHING

Weave in all loose ends and block to measurements.

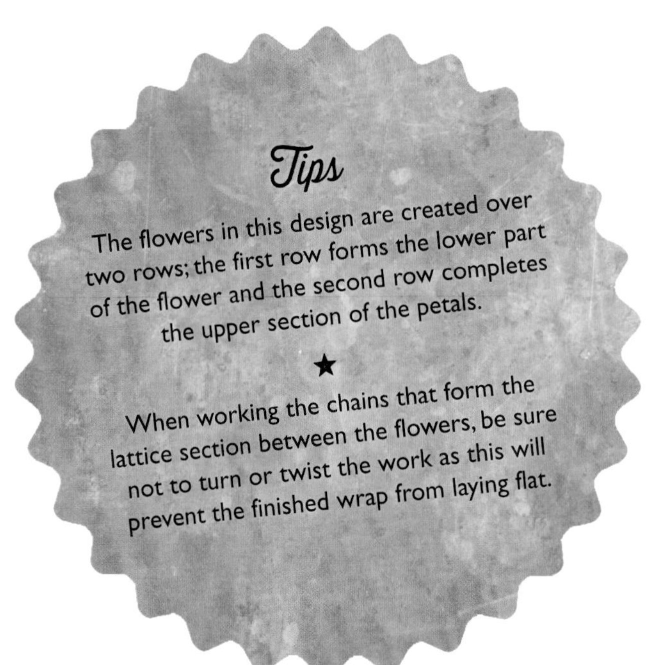

Skill Rating: ★★★

Paintbox PALETTE

Combining lace shells and pretty puff stitches, this shawl is a great way to build your crochet skills and try out new stitches. The increases along the centre line and outer edge create a swooping triangular shawl.

SPECIAL STITCHES

Puff stitch (PS): Yarn round hook, pass through stitch, draw yarn through, keeping the yarn loops long; rep from * a further 7 times (17 strands on hook). Draw the yarn through all loops on the hook, work 1ch to close the stitch.

FOR THE SHAWL

Foundation: Using 4mm (US G/6) hook, make 12ch and join with a sl st in first ch.

Row 1: 3ch (counts as 1tr), work 20tr into ring, turn. (21 sts)

Row 2: 4ch (counts as 1dtr), 1dtr in each st across marking the centre (eleventh) dtr with a locking stitch marker (see Tips), turn.

Row 3: 6ch (counts as 1tr and 3ch), miss 1 st, 1tr in next st, *3ch, miss 1 st, 1tr in next st; rep from * to end. (10 ch-sps)

Row 4: 3ch (counts as 1tr), *1PS in ch-sp, 3ch; rep from * to last ch-loop, 1PS in last ch-loop, 1tr in last st, turn.

Row 5: 6ch (counts as 1tr and 3ch), *1tr in 2nd ch of 3ch from previous row, 3ch; rep from * to last st, 1tr in last st, turn.

Row 6: 3ch (counts as 1tr), 9tr in first ch-sp, 1dc in next ch-sp, [4ch, 1dc in next ch-sp] twice, 10tr in next ch-sp, 3tr in marked centre st, 10tr in next ch-sp, 1dc in next ch-sp, [4ch, 1dc in next ch-sp] twice, 10tr in last ch-sp, turn.

Make it yours

To achieve a completely different look with this delicate lace shawl pattern, try using a heavier weight yarn and larger hook for a chunky twist.

MATERIALS

- Artesano Hand Painted Alpaca Blend (50% alpaca/50% Peruvian highland wool; 200m/219yds per 50g/1¾oz skein) 4ply-weight yarn
  3 x 50g (1¾oz) skeins in shade 78 Meadow Flowers
- 4mm (US G/6) crochet hook
- Locking stitch marker
- Tapestry needle

FINISHED MEASUREMENTS

71cm (28in) deep x 132cm (52in) wide

TENSION

1 two-row shell (one row of tr and one row of dtr) to measure 6.5cm (2½in) wide by 3cm (1¼in) long

ABBREVIATIONS

See page 9.

Row 7: 4ch (counts as 1dtr), 1dtr in each of next 9 sts, 1dc in ch-sp, 4ch, 1dc in next ch-sp, 1dtr in each of next 23 sts, 1dc in next ch-sp, 4ch, 1dc in next ch-sp, 1dtr in each of next 10 sts, turn.

Row 8: 6ch (counts as 1tr and 3ch), miss 1 st, 1tr in next st, [3ch, miss 1 st, 1tr in next st] 4 times, 3ch, miss ch-sp, 1tr in next st, [3ch, miss 1 st, 1tr in next st] 12 times, 3ch, miss ch-sp, 1tr in next st, [3ch, miss 1 st, 1tr in next st] 5 times, turn. (24 ch-sps)

Row 9: Rep Row 4.

Row 10: Rep Row 5.

Row 11: 3ch (counts as 1tr), 9tr in first ch-sp, 1dc in next ch-sp, [4ch, 1dc in next ch-sp] 3 times, 10tr in next ch-sp, 1dc in next ch-sp, [4ch, 1dc in next ch-sp] 4 times, 10tr in next ch-sp, 3tr in marked centre st, 10tr in next ch-sp, 1dc in next ch-sp, [4ch, 1dc in next ch-sp] 4 times, 10tr in next ch-sp, 1dc in next ch-sp, [4ch, 1dc in next ch-sp] 3 times, 10tr in last ch-sp, turn.

Row 12: 4ch (counts as 1dtr), 1dtr in each of next 9 sts, 1dc in ch-sp, [4ch, 1dc in next ch-sp] twice, 1dtr in each of next 10 sts, 1dc in ch-sp, [4ch, 1dc in next ch-sp] 3 times, 1dtr in each of next 23 sts, 1dc in next ch-sp, [4ch, 1dc in next ch-sp] 3 times, 1dc in ch-sp, [4ch, 1dc in next ch-sp] twice, 1dtr in each of next 10 sts, turn.

Row 13: 6ch (counts as 1tr and 3ch), miss 1 st, 1tr in next st, [3ch, miss 1 st, 1tr in next st] 4 times, [3ch, miss ch-sp, 1tr in next st] twice, [3ch, miss 1 st, 1tr in next st] 5 times, [3ch, miss ch-sp, 1tr in next st] 3 times, [3ch, miss 1 st, 1tr in next st] 12 times, [3ch, miss ch-sp, 1tr in next st] 3 times, [3ch, miss 1 st, 1tr in next st] 5 times, [3ch, miss ch-sp, 1tr in next st] twice, [3ch, miss 1 st, 1tr in next st] to end, turn.

Row 14: Rep Row 4.

Row 15: Rep Row 5.

Row 16: 3ch (counts as 1tr), 9tr in first ch-sp, 1dc in next ch-sp, [4ch, 1dc in next ch-sp] 4 times, 10tr in next ch-sp, 1dc in next ch-sp, [4ch, 1dc in next ch-sp] 5 times, 10tr in next ch-sp, 1dc in next ch-sp, [4ch, 1dc in next ch-sp] 5 times, 10tr in next ch-sp, 3tr in marked centre st, 10tr in next ch-sp, 1dc in next ch-sp, [4ch, 1dc in next ch-sp] 5 times, 10tr in next ch-sp, 1dc in next ch-sp, [4ch, 1dc in next ch-sp] 5 times, 10tr in next ch-sp, 1dc in next ch-sp, [4ch, 1dc in next ch-sp] 4 times, 10tr in last ch-sp, turn.

Row 17: 4ch (counts as 1dtr), 1dtr in each of next 9tr, 1dc in next ch-sp, [4ch, 1dc in next ch-sp] 3 times, 1dtr in each of next 10 sts, 1dc in ch-sp, [4ch, 1dc in next ch-sp] 4 times, 1dtr in each of next 10 sts, 1dc in ch-sp, [4ch, 1dc in next ch-sp] 4 times, 1dtr in each of next 23 sts, 1dc in ch-sp, [4ch, 1dc in next ch-sp] 4 times, 1dtr in each of next 10 sts, 1dc in ch-sp, [4ch, 1dc in next ch-sp] 4 times, 1dtr in each of next 10 sts, [4ch, 1dc in next ch-sp] 3 times, 1dtr in each of next 10 sts, turn.

Row 18: 6ch, miss 1 st, 1tr in next st, [3ch, miss 1 st, 1tr in next st] 4 times, [3ch, miss ch-sp, 1tr in next st] 3 times, [3ch, miss 1 st, 1tr in next st] 5 times, [3ch, miss ch-sp, 1tr in next st] 4 times, [3ch, miss 1 st, 1tr in next st] 5 times, [3ch, miss ch-sp, 1tr in next st] 4 times, [3ch, miss 1 st, 1tr in next st] 12 times, [3ch, miss ch-sp, 1tr in next st] 4 times, [3ch, miss 1 st, 1tr in next st] 5 times, [3ch, miss ch-sp, 1tr in next st] 4 times, [3ch, miss 1 st, 1tr in next st] 5 times, [3ch, 1tr in dc] 3 times, [3ch, miss 1 st, 1tr in next st] to end, turn.

Row 19: Rep Row 4.

Continue in pattern as set for a further 13 rows.

Row 33: 4ch (counts as 1dtr), 1dtr in each of next 9 sts, 1dc in next ch-sp, [4ch, 1dc in next ch-sp] twice, 1dtr in each of next 10 sts, 1dc in next ch-sp, [4ch, 1dc in next ch-sp] 5 times, 1dtr in each of next 10 sts, 1dc in next ch-sp, [4ch, 1dc in next ch-sp] 9 times, 1dtr in each of next 10 sts, 1dc in next ch-sp, [4ch, 1dc in next ch-sp] 9 times, 1dtr in each of next 10 sts, 1dc in next ch-sp, [4ch, 1dc in next ch-sp] 6 times, 1dtr in each of next 10 sts, 1dc in next ch-sp, [4ch, 1dc in next ch-sp] 4 times, 1dtr in each of next 23 sts, 1dc in next ch-sp, [4ch, 1dc in next ch-sp] 4 times, 1dtr in each of next 10 sts, 1dc in next ch-sp, [4ch, 1dc in next ch-sp] 6 times, 1dtr in each of next 10 sts, 1dc in next ch-sp, [4ch, 1dc in next ch-sp] 9 times, 1dtr in each of next 10 sts, 1dc in next ch-sp, [4ch, 1dc in next ch-sp] 9 times, 1dtr in each of next 10 sts, 1dc in next ch-sp, [4ch, 1dc in next ch-sp] 5 times, 1dtr in each of next 10 sts, 1dc in next ch sp, [4ch, 1dc in next ch-sp] twice, 1dtr in each of next 10 sts.

Fasten off.

MAKING UP AND FINISHING

Weave in all loose ends and block to measurements.

Tip

When working the puff stitch, try to maintain even loops to ensure the finished puff stitches are all a similar size, and keep the loops relatively loose so you can easily draw the yarn through all 17 loops on the hook.

Tip

The locking stitch marker should be moved up along the centre line as each row is worked; usually this will be a stitch, but sometimes it will need to be placed in the centre ch of a ch-sp.

Skill Rating: ★★☆

EMERALD *Puff*

Surround yourself in wonderful softness with this jewel coloured puff stitch wrap. These voluminous stitches are surprisingly easy to work and give this simple shaped wrap a fabulous twist.

MATERIALS

- Caron Simply Soft (100% acrylic; 288m/315yds per 170g/6oz ball) aran-weight yarn
  7 x 170g (6oz) balls in shade 9770 Cool Green (A)
  1 x 170g (6oz) ball in shade 9782 Gold (B)
- 5mm (US H/8) crochet hook
- Tapestry needle

FINISHED MEASUREMENTS

77.5cm (30½in) wide x 174cm (68½in) long

Note: This is the maximum size the wrap will block to – block to achieve a fabric you like.

TENSION

5.5 puff sts and 7.5 rows to measure 10cm (4in) over puff stitch before blocking

ABBREVIATIONS

See page 9.

Make it yours

This simple design is worked in rows; create a striped or ombré wrap by simply changing the colour of yarn every few rows.

SPECIAL STITCHES

Puff Stitch (PS): *Yarn round hook, pass through stitch, draw yarn through, keeping the yarn loops long; rep from * a further 5 times, yarn round hook and draw through all loops on the hook, work 1ch to close the stitch.

FOR THE WRAP

Foundation: Using yarn A and 5mm (US H/8) hook, make 81ch.

Row 1: 1PS in third ch from hook, 1ch, miss 1 ch, *1PS in next ch, 1ch, miss 1 ch; rep from * to last st, 1PS in last st, turn. (40 puff sts)

Row 2: 1PS in st at top of PS of previous row, 1PS in first ch-sp, *1ch, miss 1 st, 1PS in next ch-sp; rep from * to end, turn.

Row 2 sets the pattern.

Rows 3–103: Rep Row 2 for a further 101 rows. (103 rows worked in total)

Row 104: 1ch (does not count as st), 1dc in each st at top of puff st and 1dc in ch-sp between each PS.

Fasten off.

FOR THE EDGING

Using 5mm (US H/8) hook, join yarn B in any ch-sp on lower edge. Work *1PS in each ch-sp, 1ch, miss 1 st; rep from * around entire wrap and working [1PS, 2ch, 1PS] in each corner ch-sp. Join with sl st in first st.
Fasten off.

MAKING UP AND FINISHING

Weave in all loose ends and block to measurements.

Tip

Take care to maintain the length of the loops of yarn as you wrap them around the hook when creating the puff stitch to help create neat and even stitches throughout.

Tip

Puff stitch uses a large amount of yarn with each stitch. To avoid running out of yarn, count how many rows you get from the first ball of yarn A and multiply that by the total number of balls to check whether you have enough yarn to complete the number of rows worked in the main colour.

Skill Rating: ★★☆

Sparkling STARS

These sweet little stars are created with only two rounds of crochet, so they are surprisingly quick to make. What's more, the wrap is worked by joining each of the stars as you go so it will be ready to wear in no time!

SPECIAL STITCHES

Picot: Work 2ch and sl st in first ch.

FOR THE STARS

Round 1: Using 4mm (US G/6) hook, make a magic ring. Work 3ch (counts as 1tr), 11tr into the ring, join with a sl st in 3rd ch of 3ch. (12 sts)

Round 2: *2ch, 1dtr in next st, picot, work 3dc around the post of dtr, 1dc in next st; rep from * a further 5 times finishing the last repeat with a sl st in 3rd ch of 3ch from Round 1.

Fasten off and weave in ends.

Tips

The individual star motifs are joined-as-you-go, by passing the stitches from one star through the previous star as you work the picot point.

Take time to weave in the ends of each star as you finish it. It's really tempting to leave them until the end, but you'll be so glad you didn't when you finish the project!

MATERIALS

- Lion Brand Bonbons Metallics 650 Party (96% acrylic/4% metallic polyester; 35m/38yds per 10g/1/3oz ball) DK-weight yarn x 3 packs
  - 3 x 10g (1/3oz) balls in shade Yellow (A)
  - 3 x 10g (1/3oz) balls in shade Orange (B)
  - 3 x 10g (1/3oz) balls in shade Red (C)
  - 3 x 10g (1/3oz) balls in shade Brown (D)
  - 3 x 10g (1/3oz) balls in shade Silver (E)
  - 3 x 10g (1/3oz) balls in shade Turquoise (F)
  - 3 x 10g (1/3oz) balls in shade Pink (G)
  - 3 x 10g (1/3oz) balls in shade Purple (H)
- 4mm (US G/6) crochet hook
- Tapestry needle

FINISHED MEASUREMENTS

45.5cm (18in) wide x 157cm (62in) long

TENSION

1 star to measure 6.5cm (2½in) from point to point

ABBREVIATIONS

See page 9.

FOR THE WRAP

Join stars as-you-go at the creation of the picot point as follows: Work 2ch at the point of the star, pass the stitch through the picot point on the next star and work the remaining picot with sl st in first stitch and then continue working the star.

Make and join stars in the following colour sequence:

Row 1: A, B, C, D, E, F, G, H.

Row 2: H, A, B, C, D, E, F, G.

Row 3: G, H, A, B, C, D, E, F.

Row 4: F, G, H, A, B, C, D, E.

Row 5: E, F, G, H, A, B, C, D.

Row 6: D, E, F, G, H, A, B, C.

Row 7: C, D, E, F, G, H, A, B.

Row 8: B, C, D, E, F, G, H, A.

Rep this 8-row sequence three times (24 rows in total), making and joining 192 stars; 24 in each colour.

MAKING UP AND FINISHING

Weave in any remaining ends and block to measurements.

Make it yours

The colour repeat is worked by moving one star to the left on each row; mix things up by working the stars in a random design, or create solid blocks of colour with stripes.

Skill Rating: ★★☆

Zig-zag STRIPES

This casual wrap, crocheted in cool cottons, is a great accessory for festival season. Wear it draped over your shoulders for bright boho style and select vibrant shades to make the striking geometric chevron pattern.

FOR THE WRAP

Foundation: Using yarn A and 5mm (US H/8) hook, make 112ch.

Row 1: 1ch (does not count as st), dc2tog, 1dc in each of next 6 ch, 3dc in next ch, *1dc in each of next 8 ch, miss 2 ch, 1dc in each of next 8 ch, 3dc in next ch; rep from * to last 8 ch, 1dc in each of next 6 ch, dc2tog.

Row 2: 1ch, dc2tog, 1dc in each of next 6 sts, 3dc in next st, *1dc in each of next 8 sts, miss 2 sts, 1dc in each of next 8 sts, 3dc in next st; rep from * to last 8 sts, 1dc in each of next 6 sts, dc2tog.

Row 2 sets pattern.

Continue working repeats of Row 2, changing colours in the following sequence:

Rows 3–8: Yarn B.

Row 9: Yarn A.

Rows 10–11: Yarn C.

Row 12: Yarn A.

> ***Tip***
> The chevron pattern is created with simple increases and decreases worked along the row. Once you have set the chevron pattern you will find it easy to keep track of where you are by looking at the stitches worked on the previous row.

MATERIALS

- Lily Sugar 'n' Cream Solids (100% cotton; 109m/120yds per 70g/2½oz ball) aran-weight yarn
  - 4 x 70g (2½oz) balls in shade 01004 Soft Ecru (A)
  - 3 x 70g (2½oz) balls in shade 01725 Blueberry (B)
  - 3 x 70g (2½oz) balls in shade 01699 Tangerine (C)
  - 3 x 70g (2½oz) balls in shade 00084 Sage Green (D)
  - 3 x 70g (2½oz) balls in shade 01318 Blackcurrant (E)
- 5mm (US H/8) crochet hook
- Tapestry needle

FINISHED MEASUREMENTS

53cm (21in) wide x 193cm (76in) long

TENSION

14 sts and 11 rows to measure 10cm (4in) over chevron pattern

ABBREVIATIONS

See page 9.

Rows 13–14: Yarn D.
Row 15: Yarn A.
Rows 16–17: Yarn E.
Row 18: Yarn A.
Rows 19–20: Yarn B.
Row 21: Yarn A.
Rows 22–27: Yarn C.
Row 28: Yarn A.
Rows 29–30: Yarn D.
Row 31: Yarn A.
Rows 32–33: Yarn E.
Row 34: Yarn A.
Rows 35–36: Yarn B.
Row 37: Yarn A.
Rows 38–39: Yarn C.
Row 40: Yarn A.
Rows 41–46: Yarn D.
Row 47: Yarn A.
Rows 48–49: Yarn E.
Row 50: Yarn A.
Rows 51–52: Yarn B.
Row 53: Yarn A.
Rows 54–55: Yarn C.
Row 56: Yarn A.
Rows 57–58: Yarn D.
Row 59: Yarn A.
Row 60–65: Yarn D.
Rep Rows 2–65 twice more.
Change to yarn A and work two more rows in pattern as set.
Fasten off.

MAKING UP AND FINISHING

Weave in all loose ends and block to measurements.

Make it yours

Chevron patterns are the perfect opportunity to play with colour – go bold, subtle, clashing, complementary – it's up to you!

Play up the boho style and work a series of tassels along the two shorter ends to give the wrap a fringed finish.

Chapter 2

WARM AND RICH

Skill Rating: ★☆☆

Golden GLOW

Worked in a neat woven crochet stitch, the textured fabric of this cosy wrap is completely reversible and a pretty shell border adds the perfect finishing touch.

MATERIALS

- Berroco Comfort (50% nylon/50% acrylic; 193m/210yds per 100g/3½oz ball) aran-weight yarn
  7 x 100g (3½oz) balls in shade 9743 Goldenrod
- 5mm (US H/8) crochet hook
- Tapestry needle

FINISHED MEASUREMENTS

53cm (21in) wide x 185cm (73in) long

TENSION

20 sts and 16 rows to measure 10cm (4in) over woven stitch

ABBREVIATIONS

See page 9.

FOR THE WRAP

Foundation: Using 5mm (US H/8) hook, make 103ch. 1dc in third ch from hook (missed 2ch count as ch-sp), *1ch, miss 1 ch, 1dc in next ch; rep from * to end, turn. (51 sts and 51 ch-sps)

Row 1: 2ch (counts as ch-sp), *1dc in ch-sp, 1ch; rep from * to last ch-sp (the 2ch of previous row), 1dc in last ch-sp, turn.

Row 1 sets the woven stitch pattern.

Work repeats of Row 1 until piece measures 183cm (72in).

FOR THE EDGING

Round 1: 1ch, 1dc in each st and row end around entire outer edge working [1dc, 1ch, 1dc] in each corner, join with sl st in first st.

Round 2: Sl st in first st, *miss 1 st, 3tr in next st, miss 1 st, sl st in next st; rep from * to end working 6tr in each corner ch-sp. Fasten off.

MAKING UP AND FINISHING

Weave in all loose ends and block to measurements.

Make it yours

This woven stitch can be made even more dramatic by working with a chunkier weight yarn and pairing it with a larger crochet hook.

Tips

Once the first few rows of this wrap have been worked the stitch pattern is easy to remember and you can keep track of where you are by looking at the stitches on the row below.

★

This design is completely reversible – there is no wrong or right side on the finished make – so be sure to weave in all ends as neatly as possible so they are not visible from either side.

MATERIALS

- Mirasol Pima Kuri (100% pima cotton; 190m/208yds per 100g/3½oz skein) DK-weight yarn 5 x 100g (3½oz) skeins in shade 015 Apple
- 4mm (US G/6) crochet hook
- Tapestry needle

FINISHED MEASUREMENTS

86cm (34in) deep x 173cm (68in) wide

TENSION

24 sts and 8 rows to measure 10cm (4in)

ABBREVIATIONS

See page 9.

Skill Rating: ★☆☆

Green APPLES

Wrap yourself up in this classic granny triangle shawl. Based on the traditional granny square, this design is simple and stylish; worked up in a bright bold colour, it takes on a fresh modern look.

FOR THE SHAWL

Foundation: Using 4mm (US G/6) hook, make a magic ring. Work 1ch, 3dc into ring and draw up tightly to conceal the hole, creating a small half-moon shape with 3 sts. Turn and continue in rows as follows:

Row 1: 3ch (counts a 1tr throughout), 2tr in first st, 2ch, miss 1 st, 3tr in last st, turn. (2 clusters and 1 ch-sp)

Row 2: 3ch, 2tr in first st, 1ch, [3tr, 2ch, 3tr] in ch-sp (centre line made), 1ch, 3tr in third ch of 3ch, turn. (4 clusters and 3 ch-sps)

Row 3: 3ch, 2tr in first st, 1ch, 3tr in first ch-sp, 1ch, [3tr, 2ch, 3tr] in 2ch-sp, 1ch, 3tr in next ch-sp, 1ch, 3tr in third ch of 3ch, turn. (6 clusters and 5 ch-sps)

Row 4: 3ch, 2tr in first st, 1ch, 3tr in first ch-sp, 1ch, 3tr in next ch-sp, 1ch, [3tr, 2ch, 3tr] in 2ch-sp, *1ch, 3tr in next ch-sp; rep from * once more, 1ch, 3tr in third ch of 3ch, turn. (8 clusters and 7 ch-sps)

Row 5: 3ch, 2tr in first st, 1ch, 3tr in first ch-sp, 1ch, *3tr in next ch-sp, 1ch; rep from * to 2ch-sp, [3tr, 2ch, 3tr] in 2ch-sp, 1ch, **3tr in next ch-sp, 1ch; rep from ** to end, 3tr in third ch of 3ch, turn. (2 clusters and two 1ch-sps increased)

Row 5 sets pattern.

Tip

This shawl is constructed from the top down so you can measure the size against yourself as you work and adjust as desired. Increase the size by continuing the pattern as set, remembering to increase yarn amounts to accommodate a larger design.

Continue working reps of Row 5 for a further 45 rows. (50 rows worked in total – 100 clusters and 99 ch-sps)

Do not break yarn.

FOR THE PICOT EDGING

Row 1: 1ch (does not count as st), 1dc in each st and ch-sp to end, working [1dc, 1ch, 1dc] in 2ch-sp, turn.

Row 2: Sl st in first st, *[3ch, sl st in 2nd ch from hook] (picot made), miss 1 st, 1dc in next st; rep from * to end, working last st as a sl st rather than a dc. Fasten off.

MAKING UP AND FINISHING

Weave in all loose ends and block to measurements, paying close attention to the picot edging and gently pulling the points into shape.

Make it yours

Create a striped finish for the shawl by selecting a few of your favourite shades and alternating the colours every couple of rows.

Skill Rating: ★★★

WOODLAND *Colours*

Crocodile stitch creates a dramatic 3D finish to this simple triangular shawl, which is worked from the bottom upwards, making use of simple increases on each row to create the shape. Work with two contrasting shades of yarn for a bold stripe effect.

Tip

The crocodile stitch is created over two rows; the first is the foundation and the second creates the stitch. The "scales" of the crocodile stitch are off-set on each row, and after increasing on each of the foundation rows each row of crocodile stitches will have one more "scale" than the previous row.

FOR THE SHAWL

Row 1: Using yarn A and 5mm (US H/8) hook, make 7ch (first 4ch count as 1tr and 1ch), 2tr in fifth ch from hook, 1ch, miss 1ch, 1tr in last ch, turn. Note: The 2tr will now be referred to as "V-shaped tr" throughout.

Row 2: Crocodile stitch will be made by working the stitch down the first part of the "V-shaped tr" and then up the second part of the V-shaped tr as follows: 1ch, 4tr around first part of V-shaped tr working top to bottom. Rotate work and work 4tr around second part of V-shaped tr working bottom to top, 1ch, sl st with yarn B in third ch of skipped 4ch of previous row, turn. (1 crocodile st)

Row 3: 3ch (counts as 1tr throughout), 1tr into ch-sp created by last 1ch of previous row (V-shaped tr made), 1ch, 1tr in centre of crocodile st in row below, 1ch, 2tr in last ch-sp (V-shaped tr made), turn.

Row 4: 1ch, 4tr around first part of V-shaped tr, rotate work, 4tr around next part of V-shaped tr, sl st into tr, 4tr around first part of V-shaped tr, rotate work, 4tr around next part of V-shaped tr, 1ch, sl st with yarn A in third ch of 3ch of previous row, turn. (2 crocodile sts)

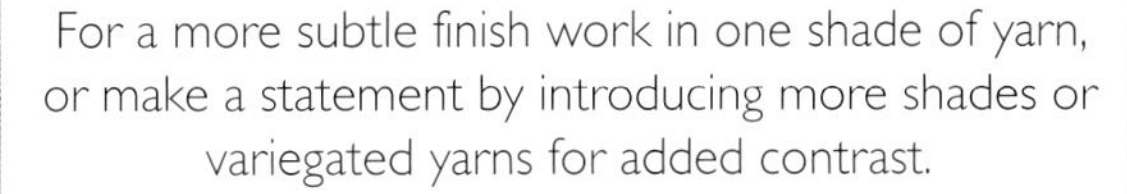

Make it yours

For a more subtle finish work in one shade of yarn, or make a statement by introducing more shades or variegated yarns for added contrast.

MATERIALS

- Cascade 220 (100% Peruvian Highland wool; 200m/220yds per 100g/3½oz skein) aran-weight yarn

  3 x 100g (3½oz) skeins in shade 7801 Rouge Red (A)

  3 x 100g (3½oz) skeins in shade 9473 Gris (B)
- 5mm (US H/8) crochet hook
- Locking stitch marker
- Tapestry needle

FINISHED MEASUREMENTS

69cm (27in) deep x 127cm (50in) wide

TENSION

1 crocodile stitch to measure approx. 3cm (1¼in) wide

ABBREVIATIONS

See page 9.

Row 5: 3ch, 1tr into ch-sp created by last 1ch of previous row (V-shaped tr made), 1ch, 1tr in centre of crocodile st in row below, 1ch, 2tr in next tr (this will be the tr from Row 3; work around the sl st from Row 4 – V-shaped tr made), 1ch, 1tr in centre of crocodile st in row below, 1ch, 2tr in last ch-sp (V-shaped tr made), turn.

Row 6: 1ch, *4tr around first part of V-shaped tr, rotate work, 4tr around next part of V-shaped tr, sl st into tr; rep from * once more, 4tr around first part of V-shaped tr, rotate work, 4tr around next part of V-shaped tr, 1ch, sl st with yarn B in third ch of 3ch of previous row, turn. (3 crocodile sts)

Row 7: 3ch, 1tr into ch-sp created by last 1ch of previous row (V-shaped tr made), *1ch, 1tr in centre of crocodile st in row below, 1ch, 2tr in next tr (this will be the tr from Row 5; work around the sl st from Row 6 – V-shaped tr made); rep from * twice more working into each consecutive crocodile st in row below and working final 2tr into last ch-sp (V-shaped tr made), turn.

Row 8: 1ch, *4tr around first part of V-shaped tr, rotate work, 4tr around next part of V-shaped tr, sl st into tr; rep from * twice more, 4tr around first part of V-shaped tr, rotate work, 4tr around next part of V-shaped tr, 1ch, sl st with yarn A in third ch of 3ch of previous row, turn. (4 crocodile sts)

Continue in pattern as set for a further 70 rows, alternating yarns, and increasing 1 crocodile stitch every 2 rows to make a total of 39 rows of crocodile sts ending with a yarn A stripe and changing to yarn B in final pull-through of last row.

FOR THE TOP EDGE

Next row: *1ch, 1dc in centre of first st, 1ch, 1dc in sp between sts; rep from * to end of row. Fasten off.

MAKING UP AND FINISHING

Weave in all loose ends and block to measurements.

Tip

This shawl can be increased in size by simply continuing in pattern as set until you have reached the desired size. Remember to increase the yarn amount accordingly.

Skill Rating: ★★☆

ROSE *Garden*

Accent a simple openwork wrap with a collection of soft luxurious crochet blooms for a truly elegant finish. The lightweight mohair yarn gives an ethereal look to this feminine design.

FOR THE WRAP

Foundation: Using yarn A and 4mm (US G/6) hook, make 129ch.

Row 1: 1tr in ninth ch from hook (counts as 1tr, 3ch-sp, 1tr), *3ch, miss 3 sts, 1tr in next st; rep from * to end, turn.

Row 2: 6ch (counts as 1tr and 3ch), miss 3 sts, 1tr in next tr, *3ch, miss 3 sts, 1tr in next st; rep from * to end, turn.

Row 2 sets pattern.

Continue in pattern as set until work measures 152.5cm (60in).

Fasten off.

FOR THE BORDER

Using 4mm (US G/6) hook and yarn B held double throughout, join yarn with a sl st in one edge. Work 3dc in each space around edge of wrap, working [1dc, 1ch, 1dc] in each corner, join with sl st in first dc. Fasten off.

Make it yours

For a more subtle finish work the wrap in a similar shade of yarn to the roses, or make a statement by making the roses in various shades for added contrast.

MATERIALS

- Debbie Bliss Rialto DK (100% wool; 105m/115yds per 50g/1¾oz ball) DK-weight yarn
  6 x 50g (1¾oz) balls in shade 065 Pale Pink (A)
- Debbie Bliss Angel (76% mohair/24% silk; 200m/220yds per 25g/1oz ball) lace-weight yarn
  3 x 25g (1oz) balls in shade 016 Blush (B)
- 4mm (US G/6) crochet hook
- Tapestry needle

FINISHED MEASUREMENTS

53.5cm (21in) wide x 152.5cm (60in) long

TENSION

[1tr, 1ch] five times + 1tr and 6 rows to measure 10cm (4in) over mesh stitch

ABBREVIATIONS

See page 9.

Tip

Mohair and lace-weight yarns can be a little bit tricky to work with – it is easy to get into a tangle and undoing mistakes can be difficult. If you are new to crochet, practise creating the roses with waste yarn before moving on to working with the mohair yarn.

FOR THE CROCHET ROSES

Using 4mm (US G/6) hook and yarn B held double throughout, make 28ch.

Row 1: 1dc in second ch from hook, 1dc in each ch to end, turn.

Row 2: *5tr in first st, sl st in next st; rep from * to end. Fasten off leaving a long tail.

Shape the roses by carefully rolling the crochet strip into a spiral with the clusters of tr sts outermost. Use the yarn tail to secure the spiral shape of the flower into position and fasten off leaving the remaining yarn tail for securing the rose to the wrap.

Rep to create a further 24 roses. (25 roses in total)

Make it yours

Create more roses and secure them more generously to the surface of the wrap for a really dramatic look.

MAKING UP AND FINISHING

Weave in all loose ends on wrap and block to measurements.

Using the photograph opposite as a guide, position six roses in a triangle formation in each of the two lower corners of the wrap and sew in place using the long yarn tails. Arrange the 13 remaining roses in two alternating rows along the lower edge – with the upper row containing six roses and the lower row containing seven roses – and sew in place.

Tip

It can be hard to conceal the ends when working on an open style stitch as used in this wrap, so try holding the yarn ends to the work as you make the stitches to secure them as you go.

Skill Rating: ★★☆

YO-YO *throw*

Crocheted yo-yos are super quick and fun to make, and by using a "join-as-you-go" method you'll be amazed at how fast this project grows! Select your favourite bright shades of cool cotton yarns to create this eye-catching striped effect.

MATERIALS

- Lion Brand Kitchen Cotton (100% cotton; 90m/98yds per 57g/2oz ball) aran-weight yarn
  4 x 57g (2oz) balls of shade 148 Tropic Breeze (A)
  4 x 57g (2oz) balls of shade 098 Vanilla (B)
  4 x 57g (2oz) balls of shade 147 Grape (C)
- 5mm (US H/8) crochet hook
- Tapestry needle

FINISHED MEASUREMENTS

51cm (20in) wide x 170.5cm (67in) long

TENSION

1 yo-yo measures 4.5cm (1¾in) across

ABBREVIATIONS

See page 9.

FOR THE WRAP

Work the first yo-yo of the first row as follows:

Foundation: Using yarn A and 5mm (US H/8) hook, make 4ch. Join with a sl st in first ch to form a circle.

Round 1: 3ch (counts as 1tr), 14tr in foundation circle. Join with a sl st in third ch of 3ch. Fasten off.

For subsequent yo-yos on first row:

Foundation: Using yarn A and 5mm (US H/8) hook, make 4ch. Join with a sl st in first ch to form a circle.

Round 1: 3ch (counts as 1tr throughout), 4tr into the circle, slip the loop off the hook and pass the hook through corresponding st on adjacent yo-yo, return loop to hook and pull-through to join, work 10tr into circle. Join with a sl st in third ch of 3ch. Fasten off.

Make a further 10 yo-yos as set, joining them to one another as you go. (12 joined yo-yos)

Make it yours

Each yo-yo requires only a small amount of yarn so this is a great way to use up oddments of yarn from your stash to create a multi-coloured design – just be sure that you select yarns of a similar weight to each other.

For the first yo-yo of second row, work as follows:

Foundation: Using yarn A and 5mm (US H/8) hook, make 4ch. Join with a sl st in first ch to form a circle.

Round 1: 3ch (counts as 1tr throughout), 4tr into the circle, slip the loop off the hook and pass the hook through corresponding st on adjacent yo-yo of first row, return loop to hook and pull-through to join, work 10tr into circle. Join with a sl st in third ch of 3ch. Fasten off.

For subsequent yo-yos on second row, work as follows:

Foundation: Using yarn A and 5mm (US H/8) hook, make 4ch. Join with a sl st in first ch to form a circle.

Round 1: 3ch (count as 1tr throughout), 4tr into the circle, slip the loop off the hook and pass the hook through corresponding st on adjacent yo-yo, return loop to hook and pull-through to join, work 5tr into circle, slip the loop off the hook and pass the hook through corresponding st on adjacent yo-yo, return loop to hook and pull-through to join, work 5tr into ring. Join with a sl st in third ch of 3ch. Fasten off.

Make a further 10 yo-yos as set, joining them to one another as you go. (12 joined yo-yos)

Second row sets pattern.

Continue in pattern, working rows of yo-yos and joining them as you go as set by the second row, to make a total of 37 rows of yo-yos, changing colours in the following sequence:

Rows 3 and 4: Yarn B.

Rows 5 and 6: Yarn C.

Rows 7 and 8: Yarn A.

Rows 9 and 10: Yarn B.

Rows 11 and 12: Yarn C.

Rows 13 and 14: Yarn A.

Rows 15 and 16: Yarn B.

Rows 17 and 18: Yarn C.

Row 19: Yarn B.

Rows 20 and 21: Yarn C.

Rows 22 and 23: Yarn B.

Rows 24 and 25: Yarn A.

Rows 26 and 27: Yarn C.

Rows 28 and 29: Yarn B.

Rows 30 and 31: Yarn A.

Rows 32 and 33: Yarn C.

Rows 34 and 35: Yarn B.

Rows 36 and 37: Yarn A.

MAKING UP AND FINISHING

Weave in all remaining loose ends and block to measurements.

Tip

Although this project is joined as you go, there are still lots of ends to weave in – try weaving them in as you finish each yo-yo to save having to do them all at the end.

Tip

The size of this wrap is easy to customise by adding fewer or more yo-yos per row, or simply by working more or fewer rows. Remember to adjust the yarn quantities accordingly to accommodate different sizing.

Skill Rating: ★☆☆

Made PEACHY

The large openwork mesh is surprisingly simple to make, worked with just chain and slip stitches, it is an ideal project for new crocheters. The design is worked from the bottom point upwards, so you can keep working until you get the desired size.

MATERIALS

- Caron Simply Soft (100% acrylic; 288m/315yds per 170g/6oz ball) aran-weight yarn
  3 x 170g (6oz) balls in shade 9754 Persimmon
  Note: Yarn is held double throughout
- 5mm (US H/8) crochet hook
- Tapestry needle

FINISHED MEASUREMENTS

90cm (35½in) deep x 200cm (78¾in) wide

TENSION

3.5 sts and 4 rows to measure 10cm (4in) with yarn held double

ABBREVIATIONS

See page 9.

FOR THE SHAWL

Foundation: Holding two strands of yarn together and using 5mm (US H/8) hook, make 9ch. Join with a sl st in first ch to form a circle.

Row 1: 9ch, sl st in foundation circle to make first loop, 6ch, sl st into foundation circle to make second loop, turn. (2 mesh loops)

Row 2: 9ch, sl st in first loop on row below, 6ch, sl st in next loop, 6ch, sl st into same loop, turn. (3 mesh loops)

Row 3: 9ch, sl st in first loop on row below, *6ch, sl st in next loop; rep from * once more, 6ch, sl st in same loop, turn. (4 mesh loops)

Row 4: 9ch, sl st in first loop on row below, *6ch, sl st in next loop; rep from * twice more, 6ch, sl st in same loop, turn. (5 mesh loops)

Row 5: 9ch, sl st in first loop on row below, *6ch, sl st in next loop; rep from * a further 3 times, 6ch, sl st into same loop, turn. (6 mesh loops)

Row 6: 9ch, sl st in first loop on row below, *6ch, sl st in next loop; rep from * a further 4 times, 6ch, sl st into same loop, turn. (7 mesh loops)

Rows 7–54: Continue in pattern as set for a further 48 rows or to desired size. (54 rows worked in total; 55 mesh loops)

Fasten off.

Tip

The mesh is created by using slip stitches to secure lengths of chain to the previous row, starting from a foundation loop. These slip stitches can be slid to the centre of each of the loops to make the mesh neat and even.

Tip

Holding the yarn double gives the stitches more density. Work with one strand from two balls of yarn at a time and ensure that you catch both yarns when working the stitches. Single balls can be re-balled into two separate balls to make working with double strands easier.

MAKING UP AND FINISHING

Weave in all loose ends and block to measurements.

FOR THE TASSELS

Cut the yarn into 184 x 30cm (12in) lengths and divide into groups of 8 strands each. Starting at the point of the shawl, feed through the loop of the mesh, aligning the ends and tie a knot to secure in place. Continue knotting the tassels at regular intervals up each side of the shawl.

(Also see page 125 for step-by-step instructions with illustrations for making tassels.)

Make it yours

The large openwork pattern of this design is well suited to cotton yarns for creating a sweet beach cover-up.

Skill Rating: ★★☆

Berries and CREAM

This super-chunky cape is worked from the bottom up and finished with a cosy roll neck. The centre section features an openwork motif for added interest and to prevent the cape from becoming too heavy.

FOR THE CAPE

Foundation: Using yarn A and 9mm (US M/13) hook, make 91ch and join with a sl st in first ch.

Row 1: 1ch (does not count as st), 1dc in each ch to end, join with a sl st in first st. (91 sts)

Row 2: 3ch (counts as 1tr), 1tr in each st to end, join with a sl st in third ch of 3ch.

Row 3: 1ch, 1dc in each st to end, join with a sl st in first st. Fasten off yarn A.

Row 4: Change to yarn B, 3ch (counts as 1tr), [1tr, 1ch, 2tr] in same st, *5ch, miss 6 sts, [2tr, 1ch, 2tr] in next st; rep from * to last 6 sts, 5ch, miss 6 sts, join with a sl st in 3rd ch of 3ch.

Row 5: Sl st in next st, 3ch (counts as 1tr), [1tr, 1ch, 2tr] in first 1ch-sp, *5ch, [2tr, 1ch, 2tr] in next 1ch-sp; rep from * to end, join with a sl st in third ch of 3ch.

Rows 6-12: Rep Row 5.

Fasten off yarn B.

Make it yours

Increase the length of the cape by working more rows of the openwork section and try it on as you go to achieve your preferred length. Remember to increase yarn amounts accordingly.

MATERIALS

- Lion Brand Hometown USA (100% acrylic; 74m/81yds per 142g/5oz ball) super-chunky-weight yarn
  - 1 x 142g (5oz) ball in shade 102 Honolulu Pink (A)
  - 2 x 142g (5oz) balls in shade 144 Seattle Sea Mist (B)
  - 2 x 142g (5oz) balls in shade 098 Houston Cream (C)
- 9mm (US M/13) crochet hook
- Locking stitch marker
- Tapestry needle

FINISHED MEASUREMENTS

106.5cm (42in) wide around shoulders x 58cm (23in) deep

TENSION

8tr and 4 rows to measure 10cm (4in)

ABBREVIATIONS

See page 9.

FOR THE SHOULDER SHAPING

Row 13: Change to yarn C, 3ch (counts as 1tr), *5ch, 1tr in next 1ch-sp; rep from * to end, join with a sl st in third ch of 3ch.

Row 14: 1ch, 1dc in first st, *5dc in 5ch-sp, 1dc in tr; rep from * to last 5ch-sp, 5dc in last 5ch-sp, join with a sl st in first st. (78 sts)

Row 15: 3ch (counts as 1tr throughout), 1tr in each st to end.

Row 16: 3ch, 1tr in each of next 14 sts, [tr2tog] twice, 1tr in next st, [tr2tog] twice, 1tr in each of next 30 sts, [tr2tog] twice, 1tr in next st, [tr2tog] twice, 1tr in each of next 15 sts to end, join with a sl st in third ch of 3ch.

Row 17: 3ch, 1tr in each of next 12 sts, [tr2tog] twice, 1tr in next st, [tr2tog] twice, 1tr in each of next 26 sts, [tr2tog] twice, 1tr in next st, [tr2tog] twice, 1tr in each of next 13 sts to end, join with a sl st in third ch of 3ch.

Row 18: 3ch, 1tr in each of next 8 sts, [tr2tog] 3 times, 1tr in next st, [tr2tog] 3 times, 1tr in each of next 18 sts, [tr2tog] 3 times, 1tr in next st, [tr2tog] 3 times, 1tr in each of next 9 sts to end, join with a sl st in third ch of 3ch.

Row 19: 3ch, 1tr in each of next 5 sts, [tr2tog] 3 times, 1tr in next st, [tr2tog] 3 times, 1tr in each of next 12 sts, [tr2tog] 3 times, 1tr in next st, [tr2tog] 3 times, 1tr in each of next 6 sts to end, join with a sl st in third ch of 3ch.

Row 20: 3ch, 1tr in each of next 6 sts, tr2tog, 1tr in next st, tr2tog, 1tr in each of next 14 sts, tr2tog, 1tr in next st, tr2tog, 1tr in each of next 7 sts to end, join with a sl st in third ch of 3ch.

FOR THE ROLL NECK

Rows 21–24: 3ch, 1tr in each st to end, join with a sl st in third ch of 3ch.

Row 25: 3ch, working in the front loops only (FLO), 1tr in each st around to create the roll, join with a sl st in third ch of 3ch. Fasten off.

MAKING UP AND FINISHING

Weave in all loose ends and block to measurements.

Tips

When joining a long foundation chain into a circle, take care to make sure the ring doesn't become twisted. You can always work the first row, then join into a ring and sew up any gaps at the start with the yarn-tail.

Autumnal colours would look just as good as the summery berry shades used for the middle and bottom of this cape.

Skill Rating: ★★☆

Roasted CHESTNUTS

Make a statement with this chunky triangular granny shawl. Mix and match your favourite multi-coloured yarn with toning solid shades, then finish with a decorative picot border for a real wow factor.

SPECIAL STITCHES

Picot: Work 2ch and sl st in first ch.

FOR THE SHAWL

Foundation: Using yarn A and 5mm (US H/8) hook, make a magic ring. Work 1ch 3dc into ring. Draw up tightly to conceal the hole and create a small half-moon shape with 3 sts. Turn and continue in rows as follows:

Row 1: 3ch (counts as 1tr throughout), 2tr in first st, 2ch, miss 1 st, 3tr in last st, turn.

Row 2: Change to yarn B, 3ch, 2tr in first st, 1ch, [3tr, 2ch, 3tr] in ch-sp (centre line made), 1ch, 3tr in third ch of 3ch, turn.

Row 3: 3ch, 2tr in first st, 1ch, 3tr in first ch-sp, 1ch, [3tr, 2ch, 3tr] in centre line 2ch-sp, 1ch, 3tr in next ch-sp, 1ch, 3tr in third ch of 3ch, turn.

Row 4: 3ch, 2tr in first st, *1ch, 3tr in first ch-sp; rep from * once more, 1ch, [3tr, 2ch, 3tr] in centre line 2ch-sp, **1ch, 3tr in next ch-sp; rep from ** once more, 1ch, 3tr in third ch of 3ch, turn.

Make it yours

This pattern is perfect for using up aran-weight leftovers from your stash to create a striking multi-coloured striped shawl.

MATERIALS

- Cascade 220 (100% Peruvian highland wool; 200m/220yds per 100g/3½oz skein) aran-weight yarn
  - 1 x 100g (3½oz) skein in shade 8311 Mineral Blue (A)
  - 1 x 100g (3½oz) skein in shade 9610 Azalea (C)
- Cascade Cherub Aran (55% nylon, 45% acrylic; 220m/240yds per 100g/3½oz ball) aran-weight yarn
  - 3 x 100g (3½oz) balls in shade 518 Roasted Chilis (B)
- 5mm (US H/8) crochet hook
- Locking stitch marker
- Tapestry needle

FINISHED MEASUREMENTS

101.5cm (40in) deep x 167.5cm (66in) wide

TENSION

26tr and 6 rows to measure 10cm (4in)

ABBREVIATIONS

See page 9.

Row 5: 3ch, 2tr in first st, 1ch, 3tr in first ch-sp, 1ch, *3tr in next ch-sp, 1ch; rep from * to centre line, [3tr, 2ch, 3tr] in centre line 2ch-sp, 1ch, **3tr in next ch-sp, 1ch; rep from ** to end, 3tr in third ch of 3ch, turn.

Row 6: Change to yarn A and rep Row 5.

Rows 7–10: Change to yarn B and rep Row 5.

Continue to repeat Row 5 alternating yarns A and B as set by Rows 6–10 (1 row in yarn A, 4 rows in yarn B), for a further 36 rows (46 rows in total), ending with a yarn A row.

FOR THE EDGING

Row 1: Continue with yarn A, work 1ch, 1dc in each st and ch-sp to end working [1dc, 1ch, 1dc] in centre line, turn.

Row 2: *4ch, miss 3 sts, sl st in next st; rep from * to end, turn.

Row 3: Change to yarn C, 1ch, [4dc, picot, 4dc] in each ch-sp to end. Fasten off.

MAKING UP AND FINISHING

Weave in all loose ends and block to measurements, taking care to draw out the points of the picots neatly.

Tips

Take time to wet block the shawl and pin out the picots along the edging to give them definition.

Make a super-sized triangle shawl by continuing the pattern as set until you reach the desired size before working the edging. Remember to increase yarn quantities accordingly.

Skill Rating: ★★☆

VINTAGE *Style*

This classic shoulder cape is constructed by seaming together colourful granny square blocks to create a neat cape that will sit smartly around your shoulders. The modular nature of the granny square makes this a great project to crochet on the go.

FOR THE GRANNY SQUARES

Block 1: Make 12 in the following colour sequence:

Foundation: Using yarn A and 6mm (US J/10) hook, make a magic ring. Work 3ch (counts as 1tr throughout), 2tr, [2ch, 3tr] 3 times, 2ch, join with a sl st in third ch of 3ch. Draw up tightly to conceal the hole. (12 sts and 4 ch-sps)

Round 1: Change to yarn B, 4ch (counts as 1tr and 1ch), *[3tr, 2ch, 3tr] in next ch-sp, 1ch; rep from * twice more, [3tr, 2ch, 2tr] in last ch-sp, join with a sl st in third ch of 4ch.

Round 2: Change to yarn C, 3ch (counts as 1tr), 2tr in first ch-sp, *1ch, [3tr, 2ch, 3tr] in next ch-sp, 1ch, 3tr in next ch-sp; rep from * twice more, 1ch, [3tr, 2ch, 3tr] in last ch-sp, 1ch, join with a sl st in third ch of 3ch.

Round 3: Change to yarn D, 1ch (does not count as st), 1dc in each st and ch-sp around, working [1dc, 1ch, 1dc] in each corner ch-sp, join with a sl st in first st. Fasten off.

Rep to make a total of 12 granny squares in this colour sequence.

Tip

Take time to block each granny square before seaming together – this will give them a more uniform shape and create a neater finish. Lay the finished squares out in the order they are to be joined to make seaming easier and to ensure you are adding the correct block each time.

MATERIALS

- Lion Brand Vanna's Choice (100% acrylic; 200m/220yds per 100g/3½oz ball) aran-weight yarn
  - 1 x 100g (3½oz) ball of shade 158 Mustard (A)
  - 1 x 100g (3½oz) ball of shade 142 Rose (B)
  - 1 x 100g (3½oz) ball of shade 102 Aqua (C)
  - 2 x 100g (3½oz) balls of shade 099 Linen (D)
- 6mm (US J/10) crochet hook
- 3cm (1¼in) button
- Tapestry needle

FINISHED MEASUREMENTS

107cm (42in) wide around shoulders x 45cm (17½in) long

TENSION

1 granny square to measure 10cm (4in)

ABBREVIATIONS

See page 9.

Block 2: Make 16 blocks in the following colour sequence:

Foundation: Yarn A.

Round 1: Yarn C.

Round 2: Yarn B.

Round 3: Yarn D.

28 granny squares made in total.

Weave in ends and block the granny squares to measurements.

FOR THE CAPE

Lay the blocks out in strips in the order shown on the illustration (right), so from top-to bottom the order is:

Strip 1: Block 1, Block 2, Block 1, Block 2.

Strip 2: Block 2, Block 1, Block 2, Block 1, Block 2.

Strip 3: Block 2, Block 1, Block 2, Block 1, Block 2.

Strip 4: Block 2, Block 1, Block 2, Block 1, Block 2.

Strip 5: Block 2, Block 1, Block 2, Block 1.

Strip 6: Block 2, Block 1, Block 2.

Strip 7: Block 2, Block 1.

Using yarn D and 6mm (US J/10) hook and with WS together, begin joining the blocks into 7 separate strips working 1dc through each corresponding stitch.

Now join the strips of blocks together in the positions shown on the illustration (right). With WS together, work 1dc through each corresponding stitch.

FOR THE SHOULDER SEAMS

With RS facing you, lay the piece down so that the row of four Block 2 squares (orientated as diamonds) is at the bottom, and the row of six Block 2 squares is at the top. On the top row, align the open sides of the Block 2 squares marked "Join" on the illustration with WS together. Using yarn D and 6mm (US J/10) hook, join with 1dc in each st, to form the shoulder seams.

Make it yours

The length of the cape is easy to adapt by simply working a few more granny squares and adding them to the bottom. Remember to adjust yarn quantities to accommodate larger sizes.

FOR THE EDGING

Using yarn D and 6mm (US J/10) hook, with RS facing, rejoin yarn in top right corner of neck edge and work 1ch, 1dc in each st and [1dc, 1ch, 1dc] at points of granny squares around entire outside edge and join with a sl st in first st.

Next round: 1ch, work 1dc in each st and [1dc, 1ch, 1dc] at points of granny squares to last st, work 12ch to form a buttonhole loop and join with a sl st in first st. Fasten off.

MAKING UP AND FINISHING

Weave in any remaining loose ends and block to measurements.

Position button to align with buttonhole loop on corresponding side of cape and sew securely in place.

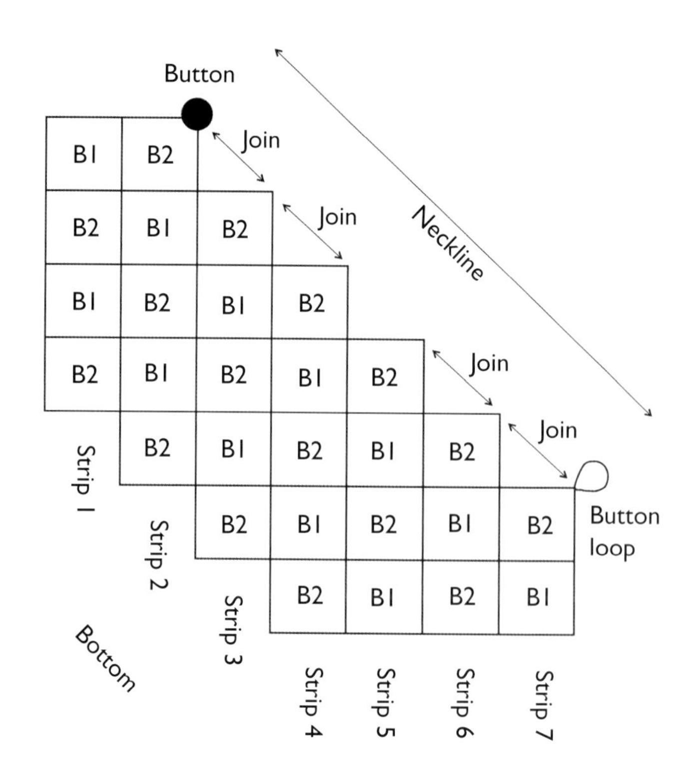

Winter BOUQUET

The open stitch patterns of this shawl are perfect for showing off colourful variegated yarns. Classic mesh stitch combined with a decorative fan-shaped edging make for a pretty and feminine finish.

MATERIALS

- Mirasol Hachito (80% wool/20% nylon; 175m/192yds per 50g/1¾oz skein) 4ply-weight yarn 3 x 50g (1¾oz) balls in shade 009 Bouquet
- 5mm (US H/8) crochet hook
- Stitch markers
- Tapestry needle

FINISHED MEASUREMENTS

62cm (24½in) deep x 152cm (60in) wide

TENSION

12dtr and 5 rows to measure 10cm (4in)

ABBREVIATIONS

See page 9.

SPECIAL STITCHES

Picot: Work 2ch and sl st in first ch.

FOR THE SHAWL

Foundation: Using yarn A and 5mm (US H/8) hook, make a magic ring. Work 5ch (counts as 1dtr and 1ch), *1dtr, 1ch into ring; rep from * twice more, 1dtr into ring. Draw up tightly to conceal the hole and create a small half-moon shape with 5 sts. Turn and continue in rows as follows:

Row 1: 4ch (counts as 1dtr throughout), 1dtr in same st, 1ch, 1dtr in ch-sp, 1dtr in next st, 1dtr in ch-sp, 1ch, 1dtr in next st and place marker in the st to indicate centre spine, 1ch, 1dtr in ch-sp, 1dtr in next st, 1dtr in ch-sp, 1ch, 2dtr in last st, turn. (11 sts and 4 ch-sps)

Row 2: 4ch, 1dtr in same st, 1ch, 1dtr in next st, 1dtr in ch-sp, 1dtr in each of next 3 sts, 1dtr in ch-sp, 1ch, 1dtr in marked st, move marker, 1ch, 1dtr in ch-sp, 1dtr in each of next 3 sts, 1dtr in ch-sp, 1dtr in next st, 1ch, 2dtr in last st, turn.

Row 3: 4ch, 1dtr in same st, 1ch, 1dtr in next st, 1dtr in ch-sp, 1dtr in each st to marked st, 1dtr in ch-sp, 1ch, 1dtr in marked st, move marker, 1ch, 1dtr in ch-sp, 1dtr in each st to last 2 sts, 1dtr in ch-sp, 1dtr in next st, 1ch, 2dtr in last st, turn.

Row 3 sets pattern.

Continue in pattern as set until you have worked a total of 26 rows including the foundation row, and shawl measures approx. 51cm (20in) deep.

Make it yours

Really show off the pretty fan border of this design by working the main section of the shawl in a variegated yarn and contrasting it with a solid colour for the lace edging.

FOR THE EDGING

Row 1: 4ch (counts as 1 dtr throughout), 1dtr in same st, 1ch, 1dtr in next st, 1dtr in ch-sp, 1dc in next st, *1ch, miss 4 sts, [1dtr, (2ch, 1dtr) 4 times] in next st (fan created), 1ch, miss 4 sts, 1dc in next st; rep from * to 3 sts before marked st, 1ch, miss 3 sts and ch-sp, work [1dtr, (2ch, 1dtr) 9 times] into marked st (centre fan created), remove marker, 1ch, miss ch-sp and 3 sts, 1dc in next st, **1ch, miss 4 sts, [1dtr, (2ch, 1dtr) 4 times] in next st (fan created), 1ch, miss 4 sts, 1dc in next st; rep from ** to last ch-sp, 1dtr in ch-sp, 1dtr in next st, 1ch, 2dtr in last st, turn.

Row 2: 4ch, 1dtr in same st, 1ch, 1dtr in next st, 1dtr in ch-sp, 2ch, 1dtr in dc, 2ch, *miss first dtr of fan, 1tr in first 2ch-sp of fan, 3ch, miss next dtr and 2ch-sp, 1dc in next dtr (central dtr of fan), 3ch, miss 2ch-sp and dtr, 1tr in last 2ch-sp in fan, 2ch, 1dtr in dc, 2ch; rep from * to centre fan, miss first dtr of centre fan, 1tr in first 2ch-sp of centre fan, 3ch, 1dc in third dtr of centre fan, 2ch, 1dc in fifth dtr of centre fan, 1ch, 1dc in sixth dtr of centre fan, 2ch, 1dc in eighth dtr of centre fan, 3ch, 1tr in last 2ch-sp of centre fan, **2ch, 1dtr in dc, 2ch, miss first dtr of fan, 1tr in first 2ch-sp of fan, 3ch, miss next dtr and 2ch-sp, 1dc in next dtr (central dtr of fan), 3ch, miss 2ch-sp and dtr, 1tr in last 2ch-sp in fan; rep from ** to last dc, 2ch, 1dtr in dc, 2ch, 1dtr in ch-sp, 1dtr in next st, 1ch, 2dtr in last st, turn.

Row 3: 4ch, 1dtr in same st, 1ch, 1dtr in next st, 1dtr in ch-sp, 1dtr in each of next 2 sts, 2ch, 1dc in dtr, 2ch, *1dc in tr, 1ch, [1dtr, (2ch, 1dtr) 4 times] in next dc, 1ch, 1dc in next tr, 2ch, 1dc in dtr, 2ch; rep from * to centre fan, 1dc in next tr, 1ch, [1dtr, (2ch, 1dtr) twice] in first dc of centre fan, [2ch, 1dtr] 3 times in second dc of centre fan, [2ch, 1dtr] 3 times in third dc, [2ch, 1dtr] 3 times in fourth dc, 1ch, 1dc in next tr, 2ch, 1dc in dtr, 2ch, **1dc in tr, 1ch, [1dtr, (2ch, 1dtr) 4 times] in next dc, 1ch, 1dc in next tr, 2ch, 1dc in dtr, 2ch; rep from ** to 2 sts before last ch-sp, 1dtr in each of next 2 sts, 1dtr in ch-sp, 1dtr in next st, 1ch, 2dtr in last st, turn.

Row 4: 4ch, 1dtr in same st, 1ch, 1dtr in next st, 1dtr in ch-sp, 1dtr in each of next 4 sts, 1dc in ch-sp, *8ch, 1dc in third dtr of fan, 8ch, [1dc in next dc, 2ch] twice, 1dc in next dc; rep from * to centre fan, 8ch, 1dc in third dtr of centre fan, 8ch, 1dc in seventh dtr of centre fan, 8ch, 1dc in tenth dtr of centre fan, **8ch, [1dc in next dc, 2ch] twice, 1dc in next dc, 8ch, 1dc in third dtr of fan; rep from * to last 2ch-sp, 8ch, 1dc in last 2ch-sp, 1dtr in each of next 4 sts, 1dtr in ch-sp, 1dtr in next st, 1ch, 2dtr in last st, turn.

Row 5: 4ch, 1dtr in same st, 1ch, 1dtr in next st, 1dtr in ch-sp, 1dtr in next 4 sts, 3ch, miss 2 sts, 1dc in dc, *[7dc, picot, 6dc] in next 8ch-sp, 1dc in dc, [7dc, picot, 6dc] in next 8ch-sp, [1dc in next dc, 2ch] twice, 1dc in next dc; rep from * to centre fan, at centre: ([7dc, picot, 6dc] in next 8ch-sp, 1dc in next dc) 4 times, **[1dc in next dc, 2ch] twice, 1dc in next dc, [7dc, picot, 6dc] in next 8ch-sp, 1dc in dc, [7dc, picot, 6dc] in next 8ch-sp; rep from ** to last dc, 1dc in dc, 3ch, miss 2 sts, 1dtr in next 4 sts, 1dtr in ch-sp, 1dtr in next st, 1ch, 2dtr in last st. Fasten off.

MAKING UP AND FINISHING

Weave in all loose ends and block to measurements.

Tips

Locking stitch markers are a great way to help keep track of the shaping as you work this pattern.

The lace design of this stitch benefits greatly from being blocked after finishing. Take time to carefully block your work, paying particular attention to the fan border, which will open up the stitches and give a professional finish.

Skill Rating: ★★★

Misty MORNING

This sweet silky cover up is worked from the yoke downward, with neat button closures. The openwork style of the mesh stitch gives the garment a floaty and feminine look.

FOR THE YOKE

Foundation: Using yarn A and 4mm (US G/6) hook, make 121ch.

Row 1: 1dc in second ch from hook, 1dc in each ch to end, turn. (120 sts)

Rows 2–3: 1ch (does not count as st throughout), 1dc in each st to end, turn.

Row 4: 1ch, 1dc in each of next 26 sts, 2dc in next st and place locking marker in first of these dc, 1dc in each of next 3 sts, 2dc in next st and place locking marker in second of these dc, 1dc in each of next 52 sts, 2dc in next st and place locking marker in first of these dc, 1dc in each of next 3 sts, 2dc in next st and place locking marker in second of these dc, 1dc in each of next 32 sts to end, turn. (124 sts)

Rows 5–6: 1ch, *1dc in each st to marked st, 2dc in marked st and move marker to first of these dc, 1dc in each st to marked st, 2dc in marked st and move marker to second of these dc; rep from * once more, 1dc in each st to end, turn.

Make it yours

Opt for a single shade of yarn for a classic finish, or select a bright shade with clashing buttons for a completely different look!

MATERIALS

- Debbie Bliss Luxury Silk DK (100% silk; 100m/109yds per 50g/1¾oz ball) DK-weight yarn
  2 x 50g (1¾oz) balls in shade 023 Lavender (A)
  2 x 50g (1¾oz) balls in shade 044 Hollyhock (B)
- 4mm (US G/6) crochet hook
- 4 locking stitch markers
- 2 x 21mm (⅞in) buttons
- Tapestry needle

FINISHED MEASUREMENTS

115cm (45in) wide around shoulders x 46cm (18in) deep

TENSION

17htr and 8 rows to measure 10cm (4in)

ABBREVIATIONS

See page 9.

Tip

Take time to carefully block your cape to open up the mesh stitch, show off the silk yarn and give a really professional finish.

Row 7: 2ch (counts as 1htr throughout), *1htr in each st to marked st, 2htr in marked st and move marker to first of these htr, 1htr in each st to marker, 2htr in marked st and move marker to second of these htr; rep from * once more, 1htr in each st to end, turn.

Row 8: Work as Row 7.

Row 9 (Buttonhole row): 3ch (counts as 1tr throughout), 1tr in each of next 2 sts, 2ch, miss 2 sts (buttonhole made), *1tr in each st to marked st, 2tr in marked st and move marker to first of these tr, 1tr in each st to marked st, 2tr in marked st and move marker to second of these tr; rep from * once more, 1tr in each st to end, turn. (144 sts)

Rows 10–12: Work as Row 7.

Row 13 (Buttonhole row): Work as Row 9. (160 sts)

Rows 14–17: Work as Row 7.

Rows 18–19: 3ch, *1tr in each st to marked st, 2tr in marked st and move marker to first of these tr, 1tr in each st to marked st, 2tr in marked st and move marker to second of these tr; rep from * once more, 1tr in each st to end, turn.

Remove markers.

FOR THE MESH STITCH SECTION

Row 20: Change to yarn B. 3ch (counts as 1tr throughout), 1tr in each st to end, turn. (184 sts)

Row 21: 3ch, 1tr in each of next 7 sts, *3ch, miss 3 sts, 1tr in next st; rep from * to last 8 sts, 1tr in each st to end, turn.

Row 22: 3ch, 1tr in each of next 8 sts, 1ch, 1tr in second ch of 3ch, *3ch, 1tr in second ch of 3ch; rep from * to last 8 sts, 1ch, 1tr in each st to end, turn.

Row 23: 3ch, 1tr in each of next 7 sts, *3ch, 1tr in 2nd ch of 3ch; rep from * to last 9 sts, 3ch, 1tr in each st to end, turn.

Rows 22–23 set mesh st pattern.

Continue in pattern as set until work measures 43cm (17in) from foundation edge, ending with Row 23.

Next row: 3ch, 1tr in each of next 8 sts, *3tr in ch-sp, 1tr in next st; rep from * to last 7 sts, 1tr in each st to end, turn.

Next row: 3ch, 1tr in each st to end. Fasten off.

MAKING UP AND FINISHING

Weave in all loose ends and block to measurements. Sew on the buttons to correspond with the buttonholes.

Tip

Silk yarns tend to be rather slippery, so be sure that all ends are securely joined and woven in to prevent them from unravelling in your finished project.

Skill Rating: ★★☆

Walled GARDEN

The Front Post treble stitch creates a wonderful texture, and a classic rectangular wrap is the perfect blank canvas for this tactile stitch design. Work with a variegated or hand-painted yarn for a really striking finish.

MATERIALS

- Caron Simply Soft Paints (100% acrylic; 190m/208yds per 113g/4oz ball) aran-weight yarn
  7 x 113g (4oz) balls in shade 0002 Rose Garden
- 5mm (US H/8) crochet hook
- Tapestry needle

FINISHED MEASUREMENTS

61cm (24in) wide x 176.5cm (66in) long

TENSION

13 sts and 8 rows to measure 10cm (4in) over waffle stitch

ABBREVIATIONS

See page 9.

SPECIAL STITCHES

Front Post treble (FPtr): Make a treble around the vertical post of a stitch on the previous row. See page 122 for step-by-step instructions.

Picot: Work 2ch and sl st in first ch.

FOR THE WRAP

Foundation: Using 5mm (US H/8) hook, make 75ch. 1tr in fourth ch from hook (missed 3ch count as first tr), 1tr in each ch to end, turn. (73 sts)

Row 1: 3ch (counts as 1tr throughout), 1tr in next st, *FPtr around next st, 1tr in each of next 2 sts; rep from * to last 2 sts, FPtr around next st, 1tr in last st, turn.

Row 2: 3ch, 1tr in next st, *FPtr around each of next 2 sts, 1tr in next st; rep from * to last 2 sts, 1tr in each of last 2 sts, turn.

Rows 1–2 set pattern.

Work rep of Rows 1–2 until piece measures 152.5cm (60in), ending after working Row 2. Do not fasten off.

FOR THE BORDER

Round 1: 1ch (does not count as st), 1dc in each st and row end around entire outer edge of shawl working 2dc in each corner, join with sl st in first st.

Make it yours

Add in a little contrast and work a few rows of plain treble stitches after each of the pattern repeats.

Tips

The texture of this stitch pattern is created by sometimes working around the front posts of stitches in the previous row, rather than working into the top of the stitch.

★

For a really neat finish, be sure to weave in all the yarn ends on the wrong side of the stitch pattern so they are less visible on the finished wrap.

Round 2: 2ch, 1htr in each st around working 2htr in each corner, join with sl st in 2nd ch of 2ch.

Round 3: 1ch, *1dc, picot, 1dc in next st; rep from * to end, join with sl st in first st. Fasten off.

MAKING UP AND FINISHING

Weave in all loose ends and block to measurements, taking care to draw out the picots.

Skill Rating: ★★☆

Old-fashioned ROSE

Wrap your shoulders in this delicate, old-rose trimmed mini-cape. Worked in the softest of silk blend yarns with an intricate fan stitch design, this is the perfect feminine cover-up for cool evenings.

FOR THE CAPE

Foundation: Using yarn A and 5mm (US H/8) hook, make 145ch.

Row 1 (RS): 1tr in third ch from hook (skipped 2ch does not count as st), 1tr in each ch to end, turn. (143 sts)

Row 2 (WS): 4ch (counts as 1tr and 1ch), *miss 1 st, 1tr in each of next 6 sts, 1ch; rep from * to last 2 sts, miss 1 st, 1tr in last st, turn.

Row 3: 3ch, 1tr in each st and each ch-sp to end, turn.

Row 4: 3ch, 1tr in each st to end, turn.

Row 5: Miss first st, 1dc in second st, *1ch, miss 4 sts, work [1dtr, (2ch, 1dtr) 4 times] in next st, 1ch, miss 4 sts, 1dc in next st; rep from * to last st, turn, leaving last st unworked.

Row 6: 1ch (does not count as st), 1dc in first st, *3ch, 1tr in first 2ch-sp of fan, 3ch, 1dc in centre dtr of fan, 3ch, 1tr in last 2ch-sp of fan; rep from * to last st, 1ch, 1dtr in last st, turn.

Row 7: 7ch (counts as 1dtr and 3ch), 1tr in first tr, 1ch, 1dc in dc, *1ch, miss next 3ch-sp, work [1dtr, (2ch, 1dtr) 4 times] in next 3ch-sp, 1ch, 1dc in dc; rep from * to last 2 sts, 1ch, 1tr in last tr, 3ch, 1dtr in last st, turn.

Make it yours

This cape is secured at the shoulder with a ribbon tie, alternatively you could create a crochet cord by working a length of chain sts then work a row of double crochet into the chain.

MATERIALS

- Louisa Harding Grace Silk Wool (50% merino wool/50% silk; 100m/109yds per 50g/1¾oz balls) DK-weight yarn
  4 x 50g (1¾oz) balls of shade 038 Dolphin (A)
  1 x 50g (1¾oz) ball of shade 052 Savon (B)
- 5mm (US H/8) crochet hook
- 130cm (51in) length of matching ribbon
- Tapestry needle

FINISHED MEASUREMENTS

107cm (42in) wide at neckline x 51cm (20in) deep

TENSION

14tr and 8 rows to measure 10cm (4in)

ABBREVIATIONS

See page 9.

Row 8: 6ch (counts as 1dtr and 2ch), 1tr in tr, *3ch, 1tr in first 2ch-sp, 3ch, 1dc in centre dtr of fan, 3ch, 1tr in last 2ch-sp; rep from * to last 2 sts, 1ch, 1tr in tr, 2ch, 1dtr in last st, turn.

Row 9: 1ch (does not count as st), 1dc in first st, *1ch, miss first ch-sp, work [1dtr, (2ch, 1dtr) 4 times] in next ch-sp, 1ch, 1dc in dc; rep from * to end, working last dc into last st, turn.

Rep Rows 6–9 twice more.

Fasten off.

FOR THE BORDER

Round 1: Join yarn B in upper right corner, work 1ch, 1dc in each st along upper edge, down first side edge, along the bottom edge and up the second side edge, join with a sl st in first st.

Round 2: 1ch, *1dc in next st, picot, 1dc in next st; rep from * to end of upper edge, 1dc in each st to end, join with a sl st in first st.

Fasten off.

MAKING UP AND FINISHING

Weave in all loose ends and block to measurements. Thread the ribbon through the eyelet holes around the neckline and trim the ribbon ends into neat angles to prevent fraying.

Tips

Take time to block your finished cape to open up and really show off the lace design. Blocking will also help to settle the silken stitches into place.

Silk blend yarns are dreamy to work with but can be a little bit slippery, so it might take a few rows of the pattern to become accustomed to their characteristics.

Skill Rating: ★★☆

On the MOORS

Wrap yourself up in this cosy crochet hooded cape. Worked from the top edge downwards, this colourful striped cape can be made to your preferred length, before adding the hood and a toggle fastening as a finishing touch.

MATERIALS

- Cascade 220 (100% Peruvian highland wool; 200m/220yds per 100g/3½oz skein) aran-weight yarn

  3 x 100g (3½oz) skeins in shade 9600 Antiqued Heather (A)

  2 x 100g (3½oz) skeins in shade 2451 Nectarine (B)

  2 x 100g (3½oz) skeins in shade 8836 Stonewash (C)
- 5mm (US H/8) crochet hook
- 12 locking stitch markers
- Toggle 4cm (1½in) long
- Tapestry needle

FINISHED MEASUREMENTS

115cm (45in) wide around shoulders x 66cm (26in) deep

TENSION

16htr and 10 rows to measure 10cm (4in)

ABBREVIATIONS

See page 9.

FOR THE CAPE

Foundation: Using yarn A and 5mm (US H/8) hook, make 78ch.

Row 1: 1dc in second ch from hook, 1dc in each ch to end, turn. (77 sts)

Rows 2-3: 2ch (counts as 1htr throughout), 1htr in each st to end, turn.

Row 4: 2ch, 1htr in each of next 4 sts, 2htr in next st and place locking stitch marker in second of these htr, *1htr in each of next 5 sts, 2htr in next st and place locking stitch marker in second of these htr; rep from * a further 10 times, 1htr in each st to last st, 2htr in last st, turn. (90 sts)

Row 5: 2ch, 1htr in each st to end, moving markers up as you come to them, turn.

Row 6: 2ch, *1htr in st to marked st, 2htr in marked st and move marker to second of these htr; rep from * a further 11 times, 1htr in each st to last st, 2htr in last st, turn.

Rows 5-6 set pattern.

Rows 7–20: Rep Rows 5–6 as set, increasing in marked sts and final st every other row and moving markers up on each row as indicated.

Rows 21–24: 2ch, 1htr in each st to end, removing markers as you come to them, turn.

Make it yours

You can omit the hood from this design and simply finish the neckline edge by continuing the border around the upper section.

Row 25: Change to yarn B. 2ch, 1htr in each st to end, turn.

Row 26: 2ch, 1htr in each st to end, turn.

Row 27: Change to yarn A. 2ch, 1htr in each st to end, turn.

Row 28: Change to yarn B. 2ch, 1htr in each st to end, turn.

Rows 29–44: 2ch, 1htr in each st to end, turn.

Row 45: Change to yarn C. 2ch, 1htr in each st to end, turn.

Row 46: 2ch, 1htr in each st to end, turn.

Row 47: Change to yarn B. 2ch, 1htr in each st to end, turn.

Row 48: Change to yarn C. 2ch, 1htr in each st to end, turn.

Rows 49–64: 2ch, 1htr in each st to end, turn.

Row 65: 2ch, 1htr in each st to end. Fasten off.

FOR THE HOOD

Foundation: Using yarn A and 5mm (US H/8) hook, make 42ch.

Row 1: 1dc in second ch from hook, 1dc in each ch to end, turn. (41 sts)

Rows 2–69: 2ch (counts as 1htr throughout), 1htr in each st to end, turn.

Row 70: 2ch, 1htr in each st to end, do not turn and work border of 70dc evenly along the long edge of the strip, turn.

Rows 71–72: 1ch, 1dc in each of next 2 sts, 1htr in each of next 66 sts, 1dc in each of last 2 sts.

Fasten off.

Next row: With RS facing, re-join yarn A at neckline edge of cape, and work 1ch, 80dc evenly across row, turn.

Next 2 rows: 2ch, 1htr in each st to end, turn.

Next row: Join one short end of hood to the neckline by working 1dc through each corresponding st, then join the other end, folding the hood so that the bordered long end is at the top (this will be the outer edge of the hood) and the unbordered edge is open at the bottom.

Re-join yarn to the base of the hood and join the two open sides together working 1dc in each st to join and create back seam of the pixie hood. Fasten off.

FOR THE BORDER

With RS facing, join yarn A at left neck, 1ch and work 1dc in each row end and st around edge of cape, changing yarn to match each colour section as you come to it and finishing at right neck.

MAKING UP AND FINISHING

Weave in all loose ends and block to measurements. Sew on toggle to neckline of cape to finish.

Tip

To get the perfect placement for the toggles, slip on the cape and pin the two parts of the toggle in position, then simply stitch in place.

Tip

The locking stitch markers will help you keep track of where to work the increases – ensure you move them up with each row that you work to keep the stitch pattern correct.

LONDON
BREWERS
HEAT

Chapter 3

NEUTRAL AND NATURAL

Skill Rating: ★★☆

Archer's COWL

Inspired by the *Hunger Games* trilogy, this quirky asymmetric cowl is ultra cosy and can easily be worn over a jacket. The super-chunky yarn works up into a rich dense fabric that holds the shape of this structured accessory.

FOR THE COLLAR AND YOKE

Foundation: With the yarn held double and 15mm or 16mm (US P/16) crochet hook, make 40ch. Join with a sl st in first ch to form a circle taking care not to twist the chain.

Rounds 1–4: 1ch (does not count as st throughout), 1dc in each st around, join with a sl st in first st.

Place a locking stitch marker on stitches 4, 17, 23 and 38.

Round 5: 3ch (counts as 1tr throughout), 1tr in each st around working [1tr, 1ch, 1tr] in each of the marked sts, join with a sl st in third ch of 3ch.

Rounds 6–7: 3ch, 1tr in each st around working [1tr, 1ch, 1tr] in each ch-sp, join with a sl st in third ch of 3ch.

Round 8: 1ch, 1dc in each st around working 2dc in each ch-sp. Join with a sl st at start of round.

Fasten off and remove markers.

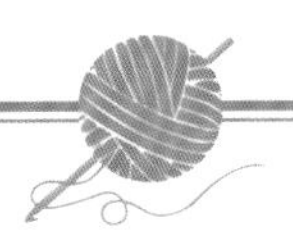

Make it yours

For a truly bold style statement, work this design in a bright colour or a variegated yarn to show off the clever construction.

MATERIALS

- Rowan Big Wool (100% wool; 80m/87yds per ball) super-chunky-weight yarn

  6 x 100g (3½oz) balls of shade 061 Concrete

  Note: Yarn is held double throughout
- 15mm or 16mm (US P/16) crochet hook
- 4 locking stitch markers
- Large-eyed tapestry needle or smaller crochet hook for weaving in ends

FINISHED MEASUREMENTS

90cm (35½in) wide around yoke x 73.5cm (29in) at longest point

TENSION

6dc and 3 rows to measure 10cm (4in) with yarn held double

ABBREVIATIONS

See page 9.

Tip

To create the ultra-cosy fabric of this accessory the yarn is held double throughout – take care to ensure you are catching both strands with the hook as you work.

FOR THE UPPER NECKLINE ON COLLAR

Re-join yarn in foundation ch at the collar.

Rounds 1–3: 3ch, 1tr in each st to end, join with a sl st in third ch of 3ch.

Fold the upper section of the collar over to the outside and pass the hook from the inside of the collar through the base of the tr sts, to work a sl st around each st to secure the rolled down section in place.

FOR THE FRONT SECTION

Foundation: With the yarn held double and 15mm or 16mm (US P/16) crochet hook, make 22ch. 1dc in second ch from hook, 1dc in each ch to end. Place a locking stitch marker on stitches 2, 10, 12 and 20.

Row 1: 1ch, 1dc in each st to end working [1dc, 2ch, 1dc] in each of the marked sts, turn.

Rows 2–4: 3ch, 1tr in each st to end working [1tr, 2ch, 1tr] in each ch-sp, turn.

Row 5: 3ch, 1tr in each st to end working 1tr in each ch-sp and moving the markers up to these tr as you work them, turn.

Row 6: 3ch, 1tr in each st to end working [1tr, 2ch, 1tr] in each of the marked sts, turn.

Row 7: 3ch, 1tr in each st to end working 1tr in each ch-sp and moving the markers up to these tr as you work them, turn.

Row 8: 3ch, 1tr in each st to end working [1tr, 2ch, 1tr] in each of the marked sts.

Fasten off.

MAKING UP AND FINISHING

Position the short edge of the Front Section along the lower edge of the Yoke between the shaping over the shoulders, with the shorter side towards the right arm. With the Front Section positioned under the Yoke join with a sl st through each corresponding stitch to join the two sections together. Fasten off.

Repeat to secure the second short end of the Front Section to the back section of the Yoke in the same manner.

Weave in all loose ends and block to measurements.

Tip

Super-chunky yarns can be tricky to fit through the eye of a needle when weaving ends in – try using a split-eye needle, bodkin or small crochet hook to make it easier.

Skill Rating: 

Shades of BLUE

This beautifully drapey shawl works with a simple colour palette – starting from a pale neutral, it moves from light through to dark blue. The addition of a simple looped edging finishes the design in true style.

MATERIALS

- Mirasol Pima Kuri (100% pima cotton; 190m/208yds per 100g/3½oz skein) DK-weight yarn
  2 x 100g (3½oz) skeins in shade 04 Cream (A)
  2 x 100g (3½oz) skeins in shade 17 Pale Blue (B)
  2 x 100g (3½oz) skeins in shade 18 Royal Blue (C)
- 4mm (US G/6) crochet hook
- Locking stitch marker
- Tapestry needle

FINISHED MEASUREMENTS

102cm (40in) deep x 220cm (86½in) wide

TENSION

17 sts and 8 rows to measure 10cm (4in)

ABBREVIATIONS

See page 9.

FOR THE SHAWL

Foundation: Using yarn A and 4mm (US G/6) hook, make a magic ring. Work 4ch (counts as 1tr and 1ch), *1tr, 1ch into ring; rep from * twice more, 1tr into ring. Draw up tightly to conceal the hole and create a small half-moon shape with 5 sts. Turn and continue in rows as follows:

Row 1: 4ch (counts as 1tr and 1ch throughout), 1tr in same st, 1tr in ch-sp, 1tr in next st, 1tr in ch-sp, 1ch, 1tr in next st and place marker in the st to indicate centre spine, 1ch, 1tr in ch-sp, 1tr in next st, 1tr in ch-sp, [1tr, 1ch, 1tr] in last st (third ch of 4ch from previous row), turn. (11 sts and 4 ch-sps)

Row 2: 4ch, 1tr in same st, 1tr in ch-sp, *miss 1 st, 1ch, 1tr in next st; rep from * to marked st, 1tr in ch-sp, 1ch, 1tr in marked st, move marker, 1ch, 1tr in ch-sp, **1tr in next st, miss 1 st, 1ch; rep from ** to last ch-sp, 1tr in ch-sp, [1tr, 1ch, 1tr] in last st, turn.

Row 3: 4ch, 1tr in same st, 1tr in ch-sp, 1tr in each st and ch-sp to marked st, 1ch, 1tr in marked st, move marker, 1ch, 1tr in each st and ch-sp to last ch-sp, 1tr in last ch-sp, [1tr, 1ch, 1tr] in last st, turn.

Row 4: 4ch, 1tr in same st, 1tr in ch-sp, *miss 1 st, 1ch, 1tr in next st; rep from * to marked st, 1tr in ch-sp, 1ch, 1tr in marked st, move marker, 1ch, 1tr in ch-sp, **1tr in next st, miss 1 st, 1ch; rep from ** to last ch-sp, 1tr in ch-sp, [1tr, 1ch, 1tr] in last st, turn.

Make it yours

Create your own ombré design by selecting two shades of your favourite colour and teaming them with a cream or neutral base yarn.

Row 5: 4ch, 1tr in same st, 1tr in ch-sp, 1tr in each st and ch-sp to marked st, 1ch, 1tr in marked st, move marker, 1ch, 1tr in each st and ch-sp to last ch-sp, 1tr in last ch-sp, [1tr, 1ch, 1tr] in last st, turn.

Row 6: 4ch, 1tr in same st, 1tr in ch-sp, *miss 1 st, 1ch, 1tr in next st; rep from * to marked st, 1tr in ch-sp, 1ch, 1tr in marked st, move marker, 1ch, 1tr in ch-sp, **1tr in next st, miss 1 st, 1ch; rep from ** to last ch-sp, 1tr in ch-sp, [1tr, 1ch, 1tr] in last st, turn.

Rows 5 and 6 set pattern.

Continue in pattern as set, repeating Rows 5 and 6, for 29 more rows. (35 rows worked in total)

Rows 36–51: Change to yarn B. Continue in pattern as set for 14 rows. (51 rows worked in total)

Rows 52–61: Change to yarn C. Continue in pattern as set for 10 rows. (61 rows worked in total)

Do not fasten off.

FOR THE EDGING

Work 6ch, miss 1 st, sl st in next st, *5ch, miss 1 st, sl st in next st; rep from * to centre st, [5ch, sl st in same st] in marked st, remove marker, **5ch, miss 1 st, sl st in next st; rep from ** to last st, 6ch, sl st in last st. Fasten off.

MAKING UP AND FINISHING

Weave in all loose ends and block to measurements.

Tip

Use a locking stitch marker to keep track of the central "spine" stitch of this shawl by placing it in the 1tr as indicated in the pattern and moving it up with each row as you work.

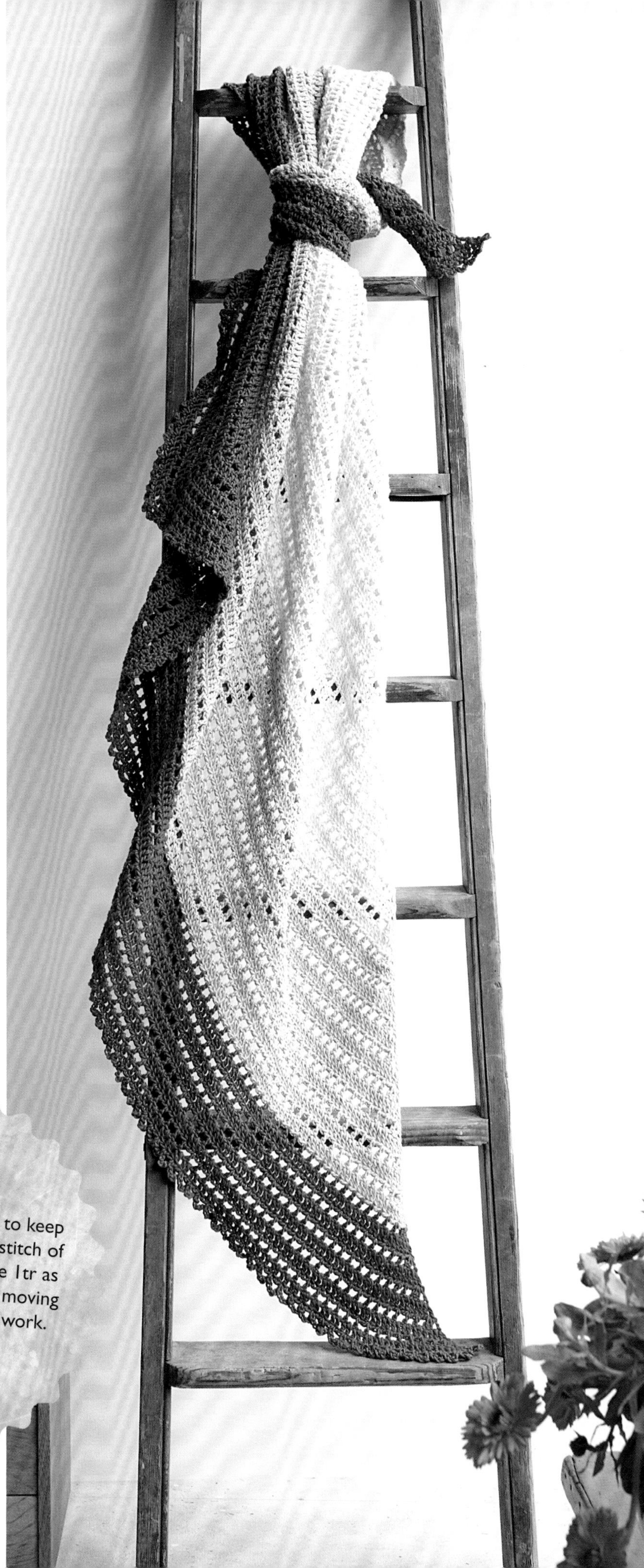

Skill Rating: 

Splash of ORANGE

Triangle stitch, based on a traditional edging stitch, is worked in neat rows here to create a modern geometric effect. Select a lightweight cotton yarn to show off the striking stitch definition.

MATERIALS

- Mirasol Pima Kuri (100% pima cotton; 190m/208yds per 100g/3½oz skein) DK-weight yarn
  - 6 x 100g (3½oz) skeins in shade 06 Midnight Pearl (A)
  - 1 x 100g (3½oz) skein in shade 08 Blazing Orange (B)
- 4mm (US G/6) crochet hook
- Tapestry needle

FINISHED MEASUREMENTS

56cm (22in) wide x 167.5cm (66in) long

TENSION

5 sts and 5.5 rows to measure 10cm (4in) over triangle stitch

ABBREVIATIONS

See page 9.

Make it yours

This striking triangle stitch gives a unique look to this wrap. Try using the triangle stitch pattern to add a decorative edging around the finished wrap and work it in a bright contrasting colour to highlight the stitches.

FOR THE WRAP

Row 1: Using yarn A and 4mm (US G/6) hook, *4ch, 1dc in second ch from hook, 1htr in next ch, 1tr in next ch (1 triangle made); rep from * a further 27 times more, turn. (28 triangles)

Row 2: 7ch, 1dc in second ch from hook, 1htr in next ch, 1tr in next ch, sl st in top of first triangle of previous row, *4ch, 1dc in second ch from hook, 1htr in next ch, 1tr in next ch, sl st in top of next triangle of previous row; rep from * to end, turn.

Row 2 forms pattern.

Rows 3–85: Rep Row 2 for a further 83 rows. (85 rows worked in total)

Row 86: 3ch, sl st in top of first triangle, *3ch, sl st in top of next triangle; rep from * to end.

Fasten off.

FOR THE EDGING

Round 1: Using 4mm (US G/6) hook, join yarn B in any ch-sp along edge. Work 1ch (does not count as st), 1dc in each st and 2dc in each ch-sp around entire wrap working [1dc, 1ch, 1dc] in each corner. Join with sl st in first st.

Round 2: 1ch, 1dc in each st around working [1dc, 1ch, 1dc] in each corner. Join with sl st in first st.

Fasten off.

MAKING UP AND FINISHING

Weave in all loose ends and block to measurements.

Tip

If you lose track of how many rows you have worked, simply count the number of triangle worked lengthways – you should have 85 triangles at the end of row 85.

Skill Rating: ★★★

River's EDGE

This cosy button-up wrap is the perfect size for throwing around your shoulders to keep wintery chills at bay. Worked on a large hook, the chunky yarn quickly transforms a dainty lace stitch into a striking modern design.

MATERIALS

- Malabrigo Chunky (100% pure merino wool; 95m/100yds per 100g/3½oz skein) chunky-weight yarn
  3 x 100g (3½oz) skeins in shade 137 Emerald Blue
- 8mm (US L/11) crochet hook
- 1 x 4cm (1½in) button
- Tapestry needle

FINISHED MEASUREMENTS

37cm (14½in) wide x 89cm (35in) long

TENSION

[1tr, 1ch, 1tr] three times and 5 rows to measure 10cm (4in) over lace pattern

ABBREVIATIONS

See page 9.

FOR THE WRAP

Foundation: Using 8mm (US L/11) hook, make 36ch. Work 1dc in second ch from hook, 1dc in each ch to end, turn. (35 sts)

Row 1: 1ch (does not count as st throughout), 1dc in each st to end, turn.

Row 2: 4ch (counts as 1tr and 1ch throughout), miss first st, *1tr in next st, 1ch, 1tr in next st, miss next st; rep from * to end, 1tr in last st, turn.

Row 3: 4ch, *[1tr, 1ch, 1tr] in ch-sp; rep from * to end, 1tr in 3rd ch of 4ch, turn.

Row 3 sets pattern.

Continue in pattern as set for a further 40 rows, or to desired length. (43 rows worked in total)

Next row: 1ch, 1dc in each st to end, turn.

Next row: 1ch, 1dc in each st to end, turn.

Next row: *Sl st in first st, 3tr in next st; rep from * to end, sl st in last st. Fasten off.

MAKING UP AND FINISHING

Weave in all loose ends, block to measurements.

Fold one of the long edges over to create the collar effect, and pass the scalloped edge border over the front to mark the position for the button before stitching the button in place.

Tip

Select a button of a size that can pass through the open weave of the stitch; this means you won't need to create a separate buttonhole and can fasten the wrap through which ever section you choose.

Make it yours

Replace the button with a classic shawl pin to hold this snuggly wrap in place around your shoulders.

Skill Rating: ★☆☆

Fields of BARLEY

This classic rectangular crochet wrap incorporates two neat keyhole openings that provide a self-fastening feature; drape the shawl around your shoulders and draw the wrap through the loops to secure it around yourself.

Tip

This is a great shawl for beginners and gives ample opportunity to practise all the basic crochet stitches. If you're unsure about how to work any of the stitches, try a few out before starting the project.!

MATERIALS

- Berroco Comfort (50% nylon/50% acrylic; 193m/210yds per 100g/3½oz ball) aran-weight yarn
  5 x 100g (3½oz) balls in shade 9720 Hummus (A)
  1 x 100g (3½oz) ball in shade 9701 Ivory (B)
- 5mm (US H/8) crochet hook
- Tapestry needle

FINISHED MEASUREMENTS

51cm (20in) wide x 172.5cm (68in) long

TENSION

12tr and 8 rows to measure 10cm (4in)

ABBREVIATIONS

See page 9.

FOR THE WRAP

Foundation: Using yarn A and 5mm (US H/8) hook, make 202ch.

Row 1: 1tr in third ch from hook (skipped 2ch do not count as st), 1tr in each ch to end, turn. (200 sts)

Rows 2-13: 3ch (counts as 1tr throughout), 1tr in each st to end, turn.

Row 14: 3ch, 1tr in each of next 19 sts, 20ch, miss 20 sts (keyhole made), 1tr in each st to end, turn.

Row 15: 3ch, 1tr in each of next 159 sts, 1htr in each ch of 20ch, 1tr in each st to end, turn.

Row 16: 3ch, 1tr in each of next 19 sts, 1htr in each of next 20 sts, 1tr in each st to end, turn.

Row 17: 3ch, 1tr in each of next 159 sts, 1htr in each of next 20 sts, 1tr in each st to end, turn.

Rows 18–23: Rep Rows 16 and 17.

Row 24: 3ch, 1tr in each of next 19 sts, 20ch, miss 20 sts (keyhole made), 1tr in each st to end, turn.

Row 25: 3ch, 1tr in each of next 159 sts, 1tr in each ch of 20ch, 1tr in each st to end, turn.

Rows 26–37: 3ch, 1tr in each st to end, turn.

Fasten off.

Make it yours

This self-fastening wrap has been worked in a single solid colour, but why not add bright stripes to make your own unique design?

FOR THE BORDER

Round 1: Using 5mm (US H/8) hook, join yarn B in any st along outer edge. Work 1ch (does not count as st throughout), 1dc in each st around working [1dc, 1ch, 1dc] in each corner, join with sl st in first st.

Round 2: 1ch, 1dc in each st around working [1dc, 1ch, 1dc] in each corner, join with sl st in first st. Fasten off.

FOR THE KEYHOLE EDGING

Using 5mm (US H/8) hook, re-join yarn B in any st in the keyhole opening and work as for the Border.

Rep for second keyhole opening.

MAKING UP AND FINISHING

Weave in all loose ends and block to measurements.

Tip

The keyhole fastening is deceptively simple to create by simply missing a set number of stitches and creating a bridging chain, but it's a technique that gives this project a really professional finish – just don't tell anyone how easy it was!

Skill Rating: ★★☆

All at SEA

Get the nautical look with this smart button-up cape. The cropped style with neat button front closures and collar is ideal for beating the chills.

FOR THE CAPE

Foundation: Using 6mm (US J/10) hook, make 70ch.

Row 1 (RS): 1ch (does not count as st throughout), 1dc in each ch to end, turn.

Row 2 (WS): 1ch, 1dc in each st to end, turn.

Row 3: 1ch, 1dc in each st to end, turn.

Row 4: 1ch, 1dc in each of next 4 sts, 2dc in next st, *1dc in each of next 5 sts, 2dc in next st; rep from * to last 5 sts, 1dc in each st to end, turn.

Row 5: 1ch, 1dc in each st to end, turn.

Row 6: 1ch, 1dc in each of next 5 sts, 2dc in next st, *1dc in each of next 6 sts, 2dc in next st; rep from * to last 6 sts. 1dc in each st to end, turn.

Row 7: 1ch, 1dc in each of next 6 sts, 2dc in next st, *1dc in each of next 7 sts, 2dc in next st; rep from * to last 7 sts, 1dc in each st to end, turn.

Row 8: 1ch, 1dc in each st to end, turn.

Row 9: 2ch (counts as 1htr throughout), 1htr in each of next 7 sts, 2htr in next st, *1htr in each of next 8 sts, 2htr in next st; rep from * to last 8 sts, 1htr in each st to end, turn.

Rows 10–11: 2ch, 1htr in each st to end, turn.

Row 12: 2ch, 1htr in each of next 8 sts, 2htr in next st, *1htr in each of next 9 sts, 2htr in next st; rep from * to last 9 sts, 1htr in each st to end, turn.

Rows 13–16: 2ch, 1htr in each st to end, turn.

Make it yours

Play up the nautical theme by working the edging with white yarn and finishing with bright red buttons.

MATERIALS

- Caron Simply Soft (100% acrylic; 288m/315yds per 170g/6oz ball) aran-weight yarn
  4 x 170g (6oz) balls in shade 9759 Ocean
- 6mm (US J/10) crochet hook
- 4 x 22mm (⅞in) buttons
- Tapestry needle

FINISHED MEASUREMENTS

117cm (46in) wide around shoulders x 38cm (15in) deep

TENSION

13htr and 9 rows to measure 10cm (4in)

ABBREVIATIONS

See page 9.

Row 17: 2ch, 1htr in each of next 9 sts, 2htr in next st, *1htr in each of next 10 sts, 2htr in next st; rep from * to last 10 sts, 1htr in each st to end, turn.

Rows 18–21: 2ch, 1htr in each st to end, turn.

Row 22: 2ch, 1htr in each of next 10 sts, 2htr in next st, *1htr in each of next 11 sts, 2htr in next st; rep from * to last 11 sts, 1htr in each st to end, turn.

Rows 23–37: 2ch, 1htr in each st, turn.

Rows 38–41: 1ch, 1dc in each st to end, turn.

Fasten off.

FOR THE BUTTON BAND

With RS facing, starting at the left neckline, re-join yarn with 6mm (US J/10) hook and work 42dc evenly down to the hem, turn.

Rows 1–2: 1ch, 1dc in each st to end, turn.

Rows 3–11: 2ch (counts as 1htr throughout), 1htr in each st to end, turn.

Rows 12–13: 1ch, 1dc in each st to end, turn.

Fasten off.

FOR THE BUTTONHOLE BAND

With RS facing, starting at the right hem, re-join yarn with 6mm (US J/10) hook and work 42dc evenly up to the neckline, turn.

Rows 1–2: 1ch, 1dc in each st to end, turn.

Row 3: 2ch (counts as 1htr throughout), 1htr in each st to end, turn.

Row 4: 2ch, 1htr in each of next 25 sts, 1ch, miss 1 st (buttonhole made), 1htr in each of next 7 sts, 1ch, miss 1 st (buttonhole made), 1htr in each of next 7 sts.

Row 5: 2ch, 1htr in each st and ch-sp to end, turn.

Rows 6–8: 2ch, 1htr in each st to end, turn.

Row 9: 1ch, 1dc in each st to end, turn.

Row 10: 2ch, 1htr in each of next 25 sts, 1ch, miss 1 st (buttonhole made), 1htr in each of next 7 sts, 1ch, miss 1 st (buttonhole made), 1htr in each of next 7 sts.

Row 11: 2ch, 1htr in each st and ch-sp to end, turn.

Rows 12–13: 1ch, 1dc in each st to end, turn.

Fasten off.

FOR THE COLLAR

With RS facing, starting at the right neck, re-join yarn with 6mm (US J/10) hook and work 70dc evenly along neckline, turn.

Row 1: 1ch, 1dc in each st to end, turn.

Row 2: 2ch (counts as 1htr throughout), 2htr in each of next 2 sts, 1htr in each of next 16 sts, 2htr in next st, 1htr in each of next 14 sts, 2htr in next st, 1htr in each of next 14 sts, 2htr in next st, 1htr in each of next 17 sts, 2htr in each of next 2 sts, 1htr in next st, turn.

Row 3: 2ch, 2htr in each of next 2 sts, 1htr in each of next 19 sts, 2htr in next st, 1htr in each of next 15 sts, 2htr in next st, 1htr in each of next 15 sts, 2htr in next st, 1htr in each of next 19 sts, 2htr in each of next 2 sts, 1htr in next st, turn.

Row 4: 2ch, 1htr in next st, 2htr in each of next 2 sts, 1htr in each of next 20 sts, 2htr in next st, 1htr in each of next 16 sts, 2htr in next st, 1htr in each of next 16 sts, 2htr in next st, 1htr in each of next 21 sts, 2htr in each of next 2 sts, 1htr in each of next 2 sts, turn.

Row 5: 2ch, 1htr in each of next 2 sts, 2htr in each of next 2 sts, 1htr in each of next 81 sts, 2htr in each of next 2 sts, 1htr in each of next 3 sts, turn.

Row 6: 2ch, 1htr in each st to end, turn.

Row 7: 1ch, 1dc in each st to end. Fasten off.

FOR THE EDGING

With RS facing, re-join yarn with 6mm (US J/10) hook at the top of the button band and work 1dc in each st and 2dc in each corner, down the button band and along the lower edge of the cape, up the buttonhole band and around the edge of the collar, join with a sl st in first st. Fasten off.

MAKING UP AND FINISHING

Weave in all loose ends and block to measurements. Sew on the buttons to align with the buttonholes.

Tips

When blocking the cape, pay close attention to the collar and button bands to ensure they lie flat and neatly on the finished garment.

Be sure that the buttons that you select are small enough to pass through the buttonholes easily without stretching them, but not so small that they slip back out.

Skill Rating: ★★☆

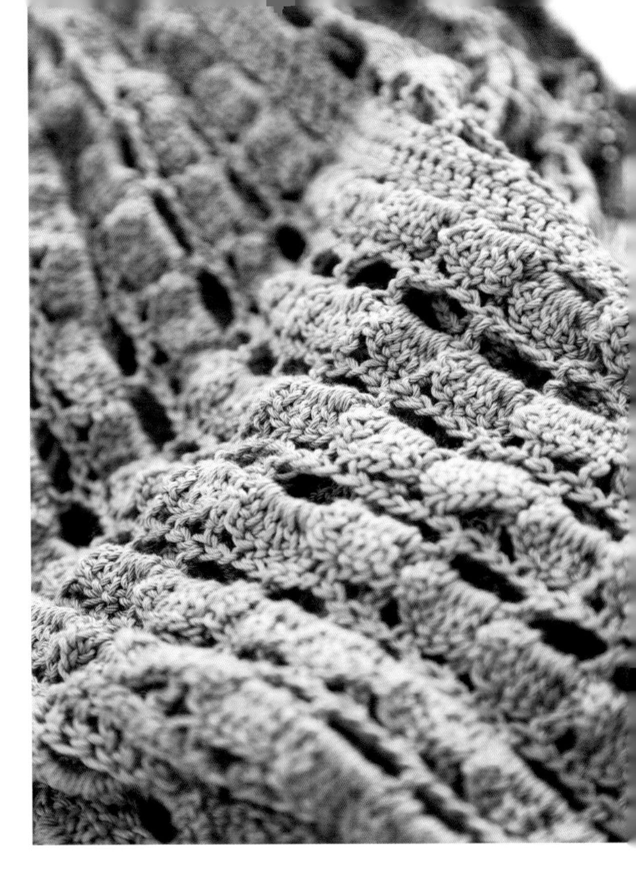

ETERNALLY *Green*

The möbius is a clever design that is looped with a twist, meaning that there is only one true surface. While this may look like a complex design, once the foundation rounds have been worked the lace is created on each side of the centre section, effectively working from the centre of the strip outwards, making it a surprisingly quick project to complete!

MATERIALS

- Rowan Cotton Glace (100% cotton; 115m/126yds per 50g/1¾oz ball) DK-weight yarn
  9 x 50g (1¾oz) balls of shade 844 Green Slate
- 4mm (US G/6) crochet hook
- Locking stitch marker
- Tapestry needle

FINISHED MEASUREMENTS

107cm (42in) circumference x 51cm (20in) deep

TENSION

[7tr-shells] 4 times and 9 rows of lace pattern to measure 10cm (4in)

ABBREVIATIONS

See page 9.

FOR THE MÖBIUS

Foundation: Using 4mm (US G/6) hook, make 201ch. 1dc in second ch from hook, 1dc in each ch to end. (200 sts)

Join the ends as follows: Lay strip flat ensuring there are no twists, and form a circle lining up the ends of the strip. Now twist one end of the strip 180 degrees to make a single twist in the strip and thus creating the möbius and join with a sl st in first st. Place a locking stitch marker to indicate beginning of round.

Round 1: 1ch (does not count as st throughout), 1dc in each st to marker, join with a sl st in first st.

FOR THE LACE PATTERN

Round 1: 6ch (counts as 1tr and 3ch), miss 3 sts, 1tr in next st, *3ch, miss 3 sts, 1tr in next st; rep from * to end, join with a sl st in 3rd ch of 6ch.

Round 2: 1ch, *3dc in ch-sp, 1dc in tr; rep from * to end, join with a sl st in first st.

Make it yours

For a cosier variation try working this design using a chunkier yarn and larger hook.

Tip

If you're unsure about how a möbius works, take a strip of paper and give it a single twist then join the ends. This will create a twisted continuous loop and it is that which forms the foundation of this shawl.

Round 3: 3ch (counts as 1tr throughout), 1tr in each st to end, join with a sl st in 3rd ch of 3ch.

Round 4: 1ch, 1dc in first st, *3ch, miss 3 sts, 1dc in next st; rep from * to end, join with a sl st in first st.

Round 5: 1ch, 1dc in first dc, 7tr in ch-sp, *1dc in next dc, 7tr in ch-sp; rep from * to end, join with a sl st in first st.

Round 6: 5ch (counts as 1dtr and 1ch), 1dc in 4th tr, 1ch, *1dtr in dc, 1ch, 1dc in 4th tr, 1ch; rep from * to end, join with a sl st in 4th ch of 5ch.

Round 7: 6ch (counts as 1tr and 3ch), 1tr in dtr, 3ch, *1tr in dtr, 3ch; rep from * to end, join with a sl st in 3rd ch of 6ch.

Rounds 5–7 set pattern.

Rep Rounds 5–7 a further 4 times, then Rounds 5 and 6 once more.

Next row: 1ch, 1dc in each st and ch-sp to end, join with a sl st in first st.

Next row: 3ch, 1tr in each st to end, join with a sl st in 3rd ch of 3ch.

FOR THE BORDER

Next row: 1ch, 1dc in first st, 4ch, miss 3 sts, *1dc in next st, 4ch, miss 3 sts; rep from to end, join with a sl st in first st.

Next row: 1ch, miss first dc *[4dc, 2ch, sl-st into 1st ch of 2ch (picot created), 4dc] in next ch-sp, miss next dc; rep from * to end and join with a sl st in first st.

Fasten off.

MAKING UP AND FINISHING

Weave in all loose ends and block to measurements – the möbius will have a natural twist in it, so it will never be able to lay flat, the twisted section can be worn at the front or side of the body as preferred.

Tip

The nature of the möbius means that after each full round you will have added the pattern to both sides of the centre strip. You can check that each round is complete by laying out the cowl and checking that the design is duplicated at each side of the centre section.

Skill Rating: ★★☆

SOFT *Summer night*

Created from a super-sized flat crochet circle with cleverly positioned armholes, this easy-make design is an elegant circular cape with a drapey shawl collar.

FOR THE CAPE

Foundation: Using yarn A and 5mm (US H/8) hook, make a magic ring. Work 2ch (does not count as st), 12tr into the ring, join with a sl st in first st. Draw up tightly to conceal the hole. (12 sts)

Round 1: 2ch (does not count as st throughout), work 2tr in each st around, join with a sl st in first st. (24 sts)

Round 2: 2ch, [1tr in next st, 2tr in next st] around, join with a sl st in first st. (36 sts)

Round 3: 2ch, [1tr in each of next 2 sts, 2tr in next st] around, join with a sl st in first st. (48 sts)

Round 4: 2ch, [1tr in each of next 3 sts, 2tr in next st] around, join with a sl st in first st. (60 sts)

Rounds 5–15: Continue as set for a further 11 rounds. (192 sts)

FOR THE ARMHOLES

Round 16: 2ch, [1tr in each of next 15 sts, 2tr in next st] 3 times, 34ch, miss next 32 sts (armhole made), [1tr in each of next 15 sts, 2tr in next st] twice, 34ch, miss next 32 sts (armhole made), [1tr in each of next 15 sts, 2tr in next st] 3 times, join with a sl st in first st.

Make it yours

This design uses varying shades of one colour to create an ombré effect; try working with variegated yarns or different plain colours for a bright bold finish.

MATERIALS

- Caron Simply Soft (100% acrylic; 288m/315yds per 170g/6oz ball) aran-weight yarn
  1 x 170g (6oz) ball in shade 9712 Soft Blue (A)
  2 x 170g (6oz) balls in shade 9709 Light Country Blue (B)
  1 x 170g (6oz) ball in shade 9710 Country Blue (C)
- 5mm (US H/8) crochet hook
- Tapestry needle

FINISHED MEASUREMENTS

132cm (52in) diameter

TENSION

12tr and 6 rows to measure 10cm (4in)

ABBREVIATIONS

See page 9.

Round 17: 2ch, [1tr in each of next 16 sts, 2tr in next st] 3 times, working into the ch work 1tr in each of next 16 ch, 2tr in next ch, 1tr in each of next 16 ch, 2tr in next ch, [1tr in each of next 16 sts, 2tr in next st] twice, working into the ch make 1tr in each of next 16 ch, 2tr in next ch, 1tr in each of next 16 ch, 2tr in next ch, [1tr in each of next 16 sts, 2tr in next st] 3 times, join with a sl st in first st.

Round 18: 2ch, [1tr in each of next 17 sts, 2tr in next st] 12 times, join with a sl st in first st.

Round 19: 2ch, [1tr in each of next 18 sts, 2tr in next st] 12 times, join with a sl st in first st.

Rounds 20–33: Change to yarn B and continue in pattern as set, join with a sl st in first st.

Rounds 34–38: Change to yarn C and continue in pattern as set, join with a sl st in first st.

FOR THE BORDER

Continue with yarn C and work 1ch (does not count as st), 1dc in each st around outer edge, join with a sl st in first st. Fasten off.

Using yarn B and 5mm (US H/8) hook, join the yarn to the armhole and work 1ch (does not count as st), 1dc in each st around, sl st at end. Fasten off. Rep for second armhole.

MAKING UP AND FINISHING

Weave in all loose ends and block to measurements.

Tips

The circle is kept flat by working the same number of increases at the same place on each round. You can check where you are on the pattern by looking at the row below.

To help keep track of the increase points, place a locking stitch marker in the stitch where the increase happens and move it up with each round.

BREWERS
HEAT

Tips

This shawl is worked in a woven crochet stitch made up of only chains and double crochet stitches, so it is an ideal project for beginners. The double crochet stitches are worked into the chain spaces of the previous row, which makes the pattern easy to master.

★

When working with different fibres, be sure to work a tension swatch in each to ensure your hook creates the same stitch size for each of the yarns selected.

Skill Rating: ★☆☆

Night SKY

Create a clever triangular shawl of contrasting textured halves. The texture of the woven crochet stitch is played up by using two different yarns, a cotton and a silk blend. Using only double crochet and chain stitches, this design is ideal for novices or those looking for a quick gift make.

FOR THE SHAWL

Foundation: Using yarn A and 4mm (US G/6) hook, make a magic ring. Work 2ch (counts as turning ch and 1dc), 2dc into ring. Draw up tightly to conceal the hole and create a small half-moon shape with 3 sts. Turn and continue in rows as follows:

Row 1: 1ch (does not count as st throughout), 2dc in first st, 1ch, 1dc in next st, 1ch, 2dc in last st, turn. (5dc, 2 ch-sps)

Row 2: 1ch, 2dc in first st, 1ch, 1dc in ch-sp, 1ch, 1dc in ch-sp, 1ch, 2dc in last st, turn. (6dc, 3 ch-sps)

Row 3: 1ch, 2dc in first st, 1ch, 1dc in ch-sp, 1ch, 1dc in ch-sp, 1ch, 1dc in ch-sp, 1ch, 2dc in last st, turn. (7dc, 4 ch-sps)

Row 4: 1ch, 2dc in first st, work [1ch, 1dc in ch-sp] to last st, 1ch, 2dc in last st, turn. (8dc, 5 ch-sps)

Row 4 sets pattern.

Continue in pattern as set, increasing 1dc and 1ch-sp every row, for a further 98 rows. (103 rows worked in total, including foundation row)

Next row: Change to yarn B and work in pattern as set for a further 54 rows.

Fasten off.

MAKING UP AND FINISHING

Weave in all loose ends and block to measurements.

Make it yours

For a more striking look, work with two highly contrasting shades, such as a neutral with a bright pop of colour.

MATERIALS

- Sublime Egyptian Cotton DK (100% cotton; 100m/115yds per 50g/1¾oz ball) DK-weight yarn
  5 x 50g (1¾oz) balls in shade 0387 Dusty Blue (A)
- Sublime Cotton Silk DK (75% cotton/25% silk; 125m/137yds per 50g/1¾oz ball) DK-weight yarn
  5 x 50g (1¾oz) balls in shade 442 Indigo Leaf (B)
- 4mm (US G/6) crochet hook
- Tapestry needle

FINISHED MEASUREMENTS

142.5cm (56in) wide x 86.5cm (34in) deep

TENSION

26 sts and 21 rows to measure 10cm (4in) over woven stitch pattern

ABBREVIATIONS

See page 9.

Skill Rating: ★★★

By the LAKE

Wrap yourself up and beat the chills with this oversized rectangular shawl. The simple design uses only five different stitches making it ideal for beginners, and worked on a large hook you'll be finished in no time! Large feature buttons keep it secure around your shoulders.

MATERIALS

- Lion Brand Unique (100% acrylic; 100m/109yds per 100g/3½oz ball) chunky-weight yarn
  11 x 100g (3½oz) balls of shade 202 Oceania
- 9mm (US M/13) crochet hook
- Locking stitch markers or safety pins for button placement
- 4 x 5cm (2in) wooden buttons
- Tapestry needle

FINISHED MEASUREMENTS

76.5cm (30in) wide x 216cm (85in) long

TENSION

8tr and 4 rows to measure 10cm (4in)

ABBREVIATIONS

See page 9.

FOR THE SHAWL

Foundation: Using 9mm (US M/13) hook, make 171ch. 1dc in second ch from hook, 1dc in each ch to end, turn. (170 sts)

Row 1: 2ch (counts as 1htr), 1htr in each st to end, turn.

Row 2: 3ch (counts as 1tr), 1tr in each st to end, turn.

Row 3: 1ch (does not count as st), 1dc in each st to end, turn.

Row 4: 2ch (counts as 1htr), 1htr in each st to end, turn.

Row 5: 3ch (counts as 1tr), 1tr in each st to end, turn.

Rows 3–5 set the pattern.

Continue as set working repeats of Rows 3–5 for a further 33 rows (39 rows worked in total including foundation row).

FOR THE BUTTONHOLE BAND

Row 41: 4ch (counts as 1dtr), 1dtr in each st to end, turn.

Row 42: 1ch, 1dc in each st to end. Fasten off.

MAKING UP AND FINISHING

Weave in all loose ends and block to measurements.

Wrap the shawl around yourself and decide on placement of the buttons (see Tips) then stitch securely in place.

Make it yours

This cosy shawl is created using a repeated pattern of three rows of stitches. Create different looks by working in stripes of solid colours or combine a solid with a variegated yarn.

Tips

The buttons are fastened through the holes created in the row of double treble stitches, so once you've decided on the placement of the buttons you can fasten it however you like. Wrap the shawl around you to decide on button placement and place a locking stitch marker to indicate where to stitch the button.

★

Ensure the buttons are small enough to fit through the rows of double treble stitches, but not so small that they slip back through!

TECHNIQUES

TECHNIQUES

In this section, we explain how to master the simple crochet and finishing techniques that you need to make the projects in this book.

Holding the hook

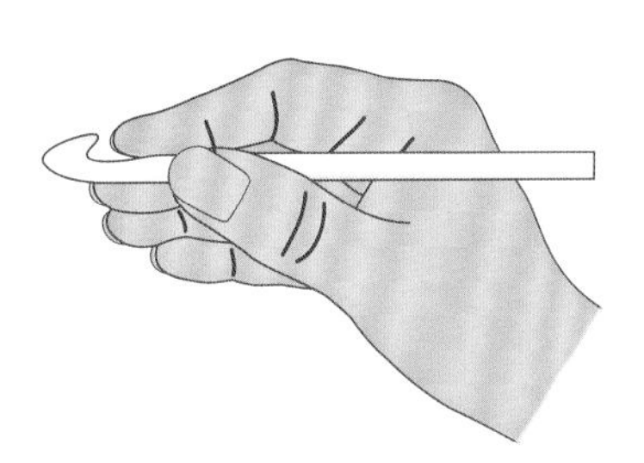

Pick up your hook as though you are picking up a pen or pencil. Keeping the hook held loosely between your fingers and thumb, turn your hand so that the palm is facing up and the hook is balanced in your hand and resting in the space between your index finger and your thumb.

Holding the yarn

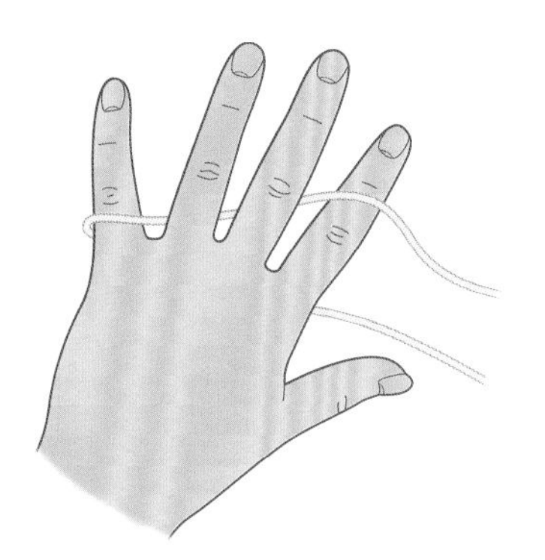

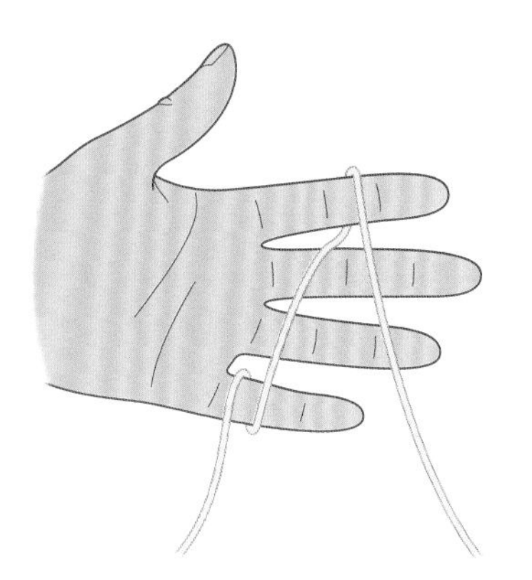

1. Pick up the yarn with your little finger in the opposite hand to your hook, with your palm facing upward and with the short end in front. Turn your hand to face downward, with the yarn on top of your index finger and under the other two fingers and wrapped right around the little finger, as shown above.

2. Turn your hand to face you, ready to hold the work in your middle finger and thumb. Keeping your index finger only at a slight curve, hold the work or the slip knot using the same hand, between your middle finger and your thumb and just below the crochet hook and loop/s on the hook.

Making a slip knot

The simplest way is to make a circle with the yarn, so that the loop is facing downward.

1. In one hand hold the circle at the top where the yarn crosses, and let the tail drop down at the back so that it falls across the centre of the loop. With your free hand or the tip of a crochet hook, pull a loop through the circle.

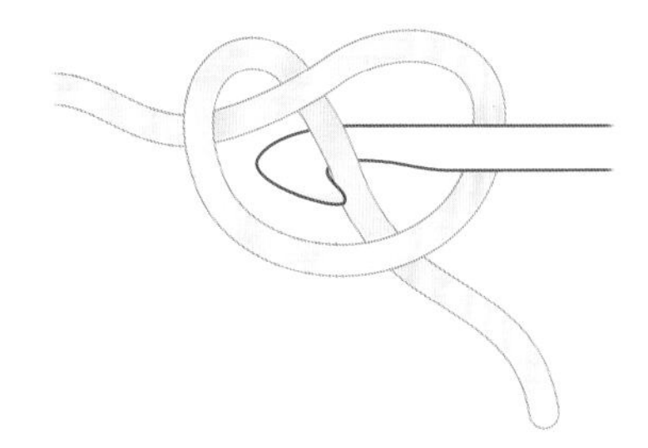

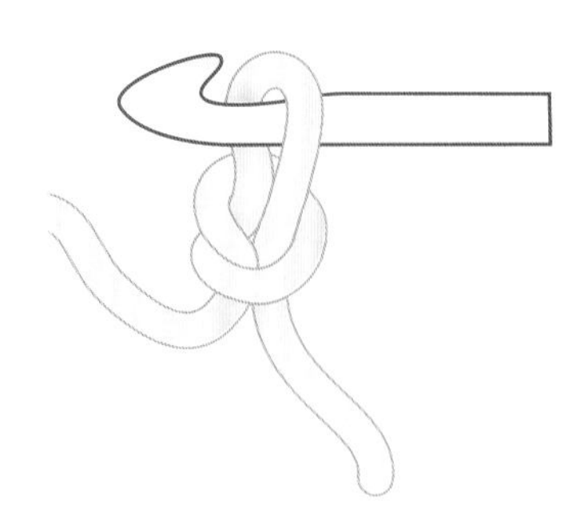

2. Put the hook into the loop and pull gently so that it forms a loose loop on the hook.

Yarn round hook (yrh)

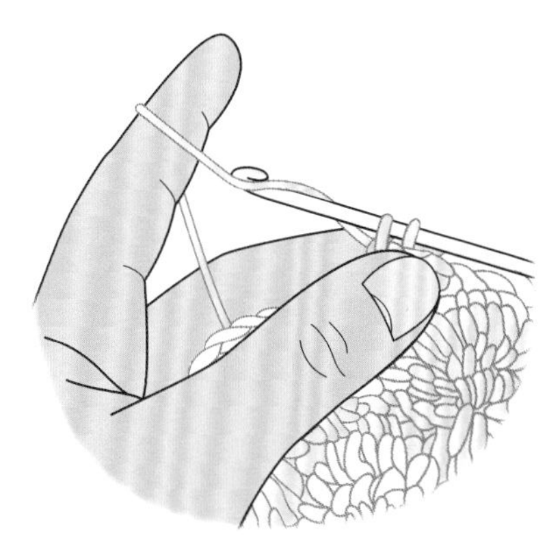

To create a stitch, catch the yarn from behind with the hook pointing upward. As you gently pull the yarn through the loop on the hook, turn the hook so it faces downward and slide the yarn through the loop. The loop on the hook should be kept loose enough for the hook to slide through easily.

Magic ring

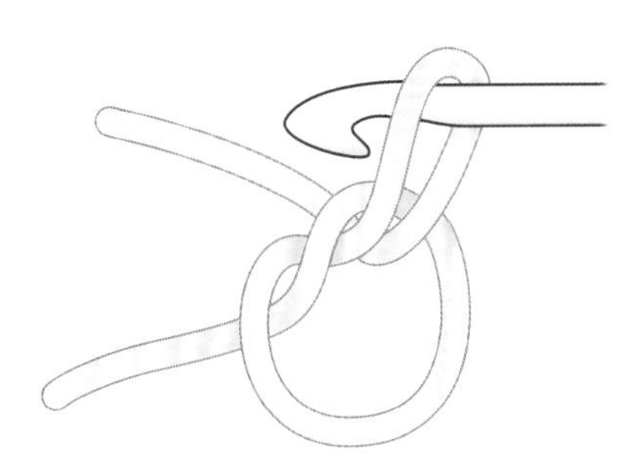

This is a useful starting technique if you do not want a visible hole in the centre of your round. Loop the yarn around your finger, insert the hook through the ring, yarn round hook, and pull through the ring to make the first chain. Work the number of stitches required into the ring and then pull the end to tighten the centre ring and close the hole.

Chain (ch)

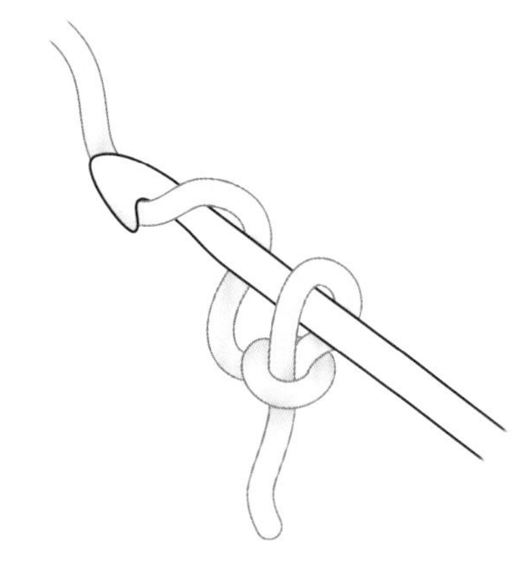

1. Using the hook, wrap the yarn over the hook ready to pull it through the loop on the hook.

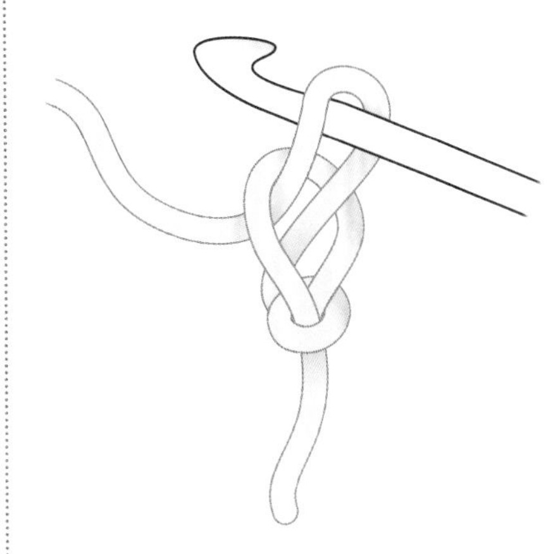

2. Pull through, creating a new loop on the hook. Continue in this way to create a chain of the required length.

Chain ring

If you are crocheting a round shape, one way of starting off is by crocheting a number of chains following the instructions in your pattern, and then joining them into a circle.

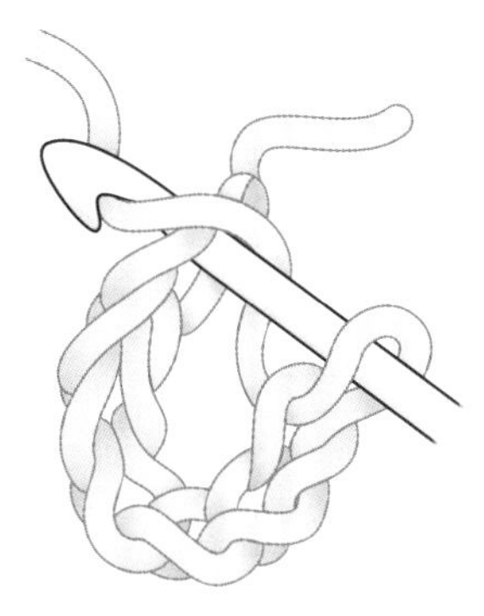

1. To join the chain into a circle, insert the crochet hook into the first chain that you made (not into the slip knot), yarn round hook.

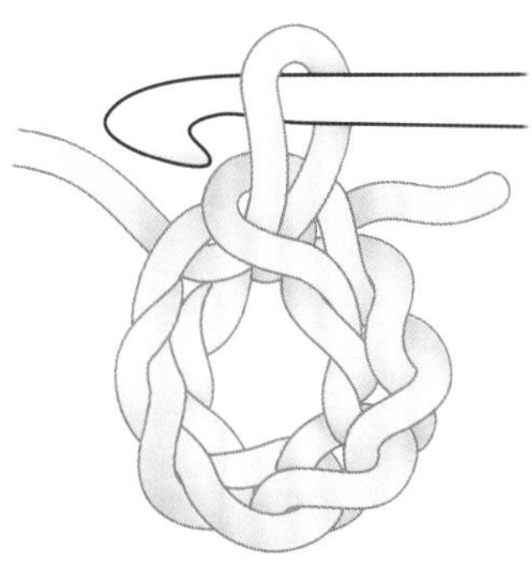

2. Pull the yarn through the chain and through the loop on your hook at the same time, thereby creating a slip stitch and forming a circle. You now have a chain ring ready to work stitches into as instructed in the pattern.

Chain space (ch-sp)

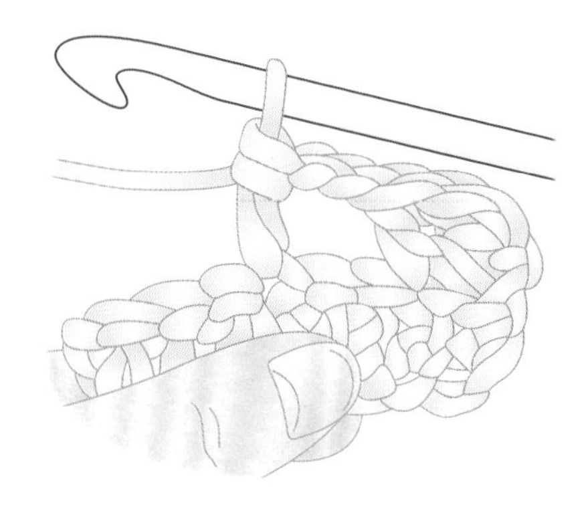

1. A chain space is the space that has been made under a chain in the previous round or row, and falls in between other stitches.

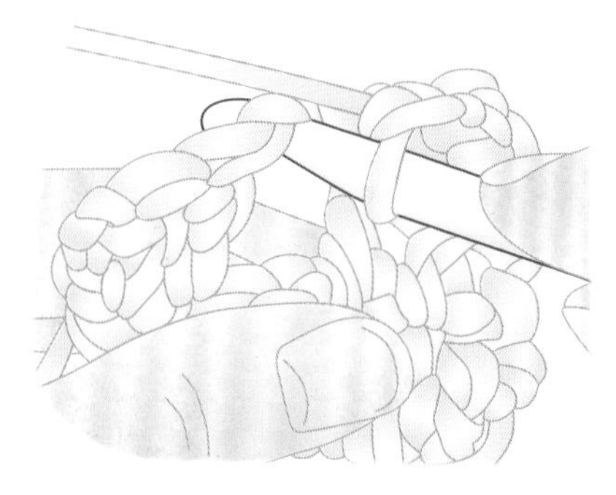

2. Stitches into a chain space are made directly into the hole created under the chain and not into the chain stitches themselves.

Slip stitch (sl st)

A slip stitch doesn't create any height and is often used as the last stitch to create a smooth and even round or row.

1. To make a slip stitch: first put the hook through the work, yarn round hook.

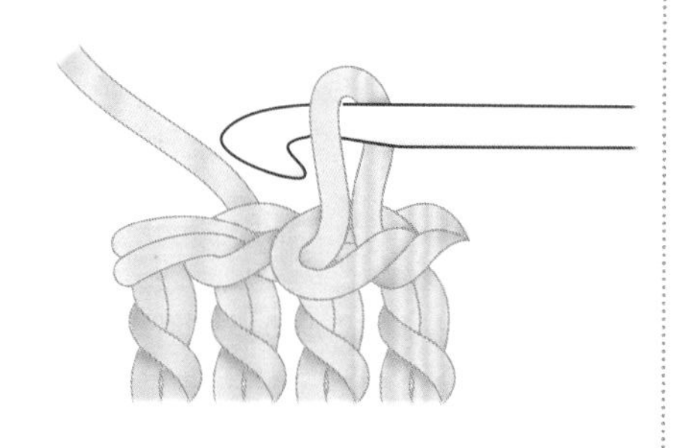

2. Pull the yarn through both the work and through the loop on the hook at the same time, so you will have 1 loop on the hook.

Making rounds

When working in rounds the work is not turned, so you are always working from one side. Depending on the pattern you are working, a "round" can be square. Start each round by making one or more chains to create the height you need for the stitch you are working:

Double crochet = 1 chain
Half treble crochet = 2 chains
Treble crochet = 3 chains

Work the required stitches to complete the round. At the end of the round, slip stitch into the top of the chain to close the round.

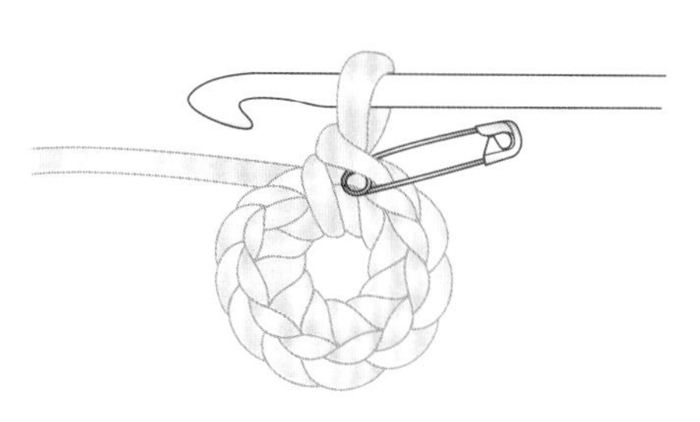

If you work in a spiral you do not need a turning chain. After completing the base ring, place a stitch marker in the first stitch and then continue to crochet around. When you have made a round and reached the point where the stitch marker is, work this stitch, take out the stitch marker from the previous round and put it back into the first stitch of the new round. A safety pin or piece of yarn in a contrasting colour is a good stitch marker.

How to measure a tension square

Using the hook and the yarn recommended in the pattern, make a number of chains to measure approximately 15cm (6in). Working in the stitch pattern given for the tension measurements, work enough rows to form a square. Fasten off.

Take a ruler, place it horizontally across the square, and using pins, mark a 10cm (4in) area. Repeat vertically to form a 10cm (4in) square on the fabric.

Count the number of stitches across, and the number of rows within the square, and compare against the tension given in the pattern.

If your numbers match the pattern then use this size hook and yarn for your project. If you have more stitches, then your tension is tighter than recommended and you need to use a larger hook. If you have fewer stitches, then your tension is looser and you will need a smaller hook.

Make tension squares using different size hooks until you have matched the tension in the pattern, and use this hook to make the project.

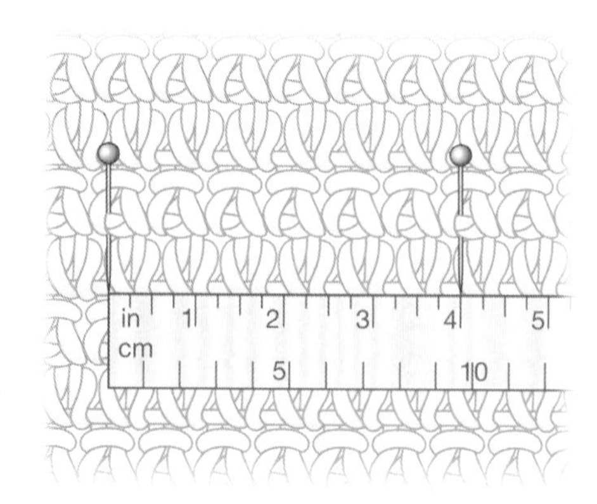

Making rows

When making straight rows you turn the work at the end of each row and make a turning chain to create the height you need for the stitch you are working with, as for making rounds.

Working into top of stitch

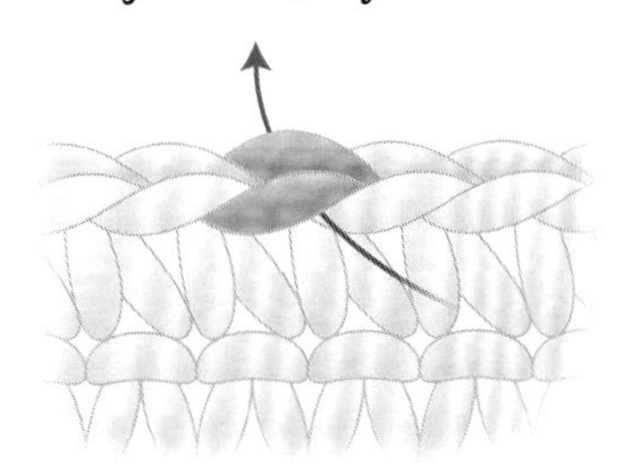

Unless otherwise directed, insert the hook under both of the two loops on top of the stitch – this is the standard technique.

Working into front loop of stitch

(FLO)

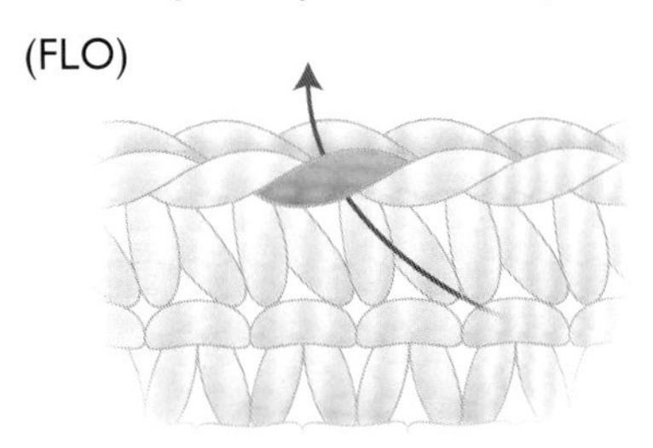

To work into the front loop of a stitch, pick up the front loop from underneath at the front of the work.

Working into back loop of stitch

(BLO)

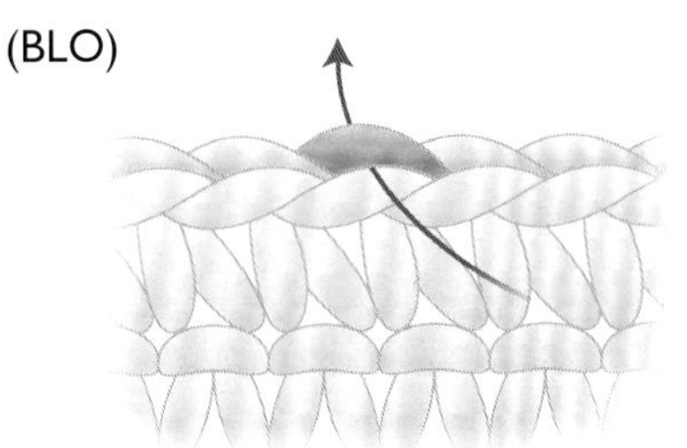

To work into the back loop of the stitch, insert the hook between the front and the back loop, picking up the back loop from the front of the work.

Double crochet (dc)

1. Insert the hook into your work, yarn round hook and pull the yarn through the work only. You will then have 2 loops on the hook.

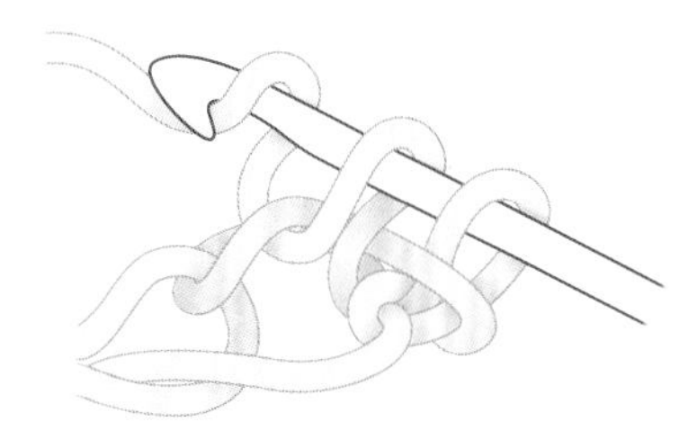

2. Yarn round hook again and pull through the two loops on the hook. You will then have 1 loop on the hook.

Joining new yarn

If using double crochet to join in a new yarn, insert the hook as normal into the stitch, using the original yarn, and pull a loop through. Drop the old yarn and pick up the new yarn. Wrap the new yarn round the hook and pull it through the two loops on the hook.

Half treble crochet (htr)

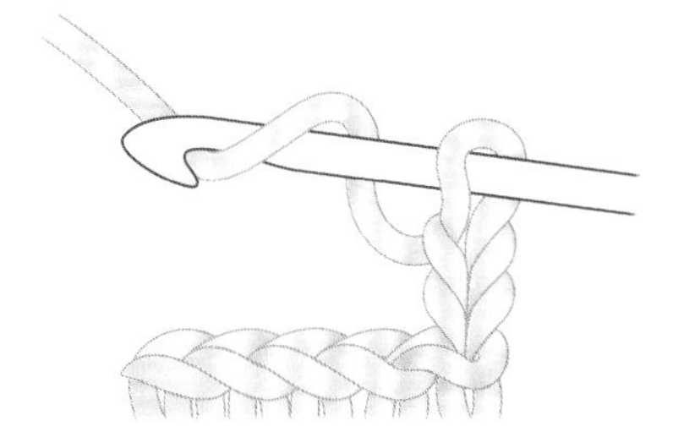

1. Before inserting the hook into the work, wrap the yarn round the hook and put the hook through the work with the yarn wrapped around.

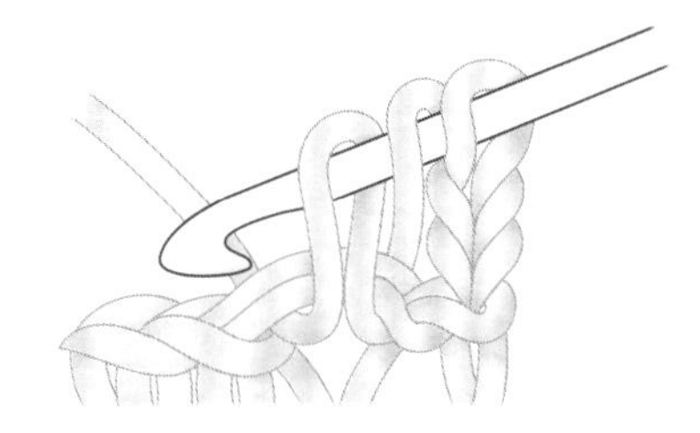

2. Yarn round hook again and pull through the first loop on the hook. You now have 3 loops on the hook.

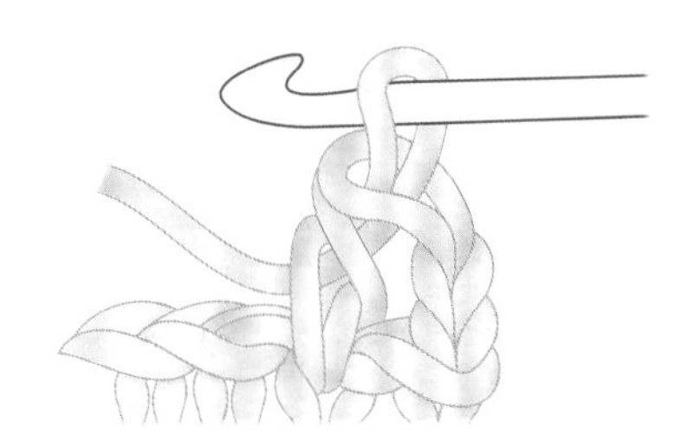

3. Yarn round hook and pull the yarn through all 3 loops. You will be left with 1 loop on the hook.

Treble crochet (tr)

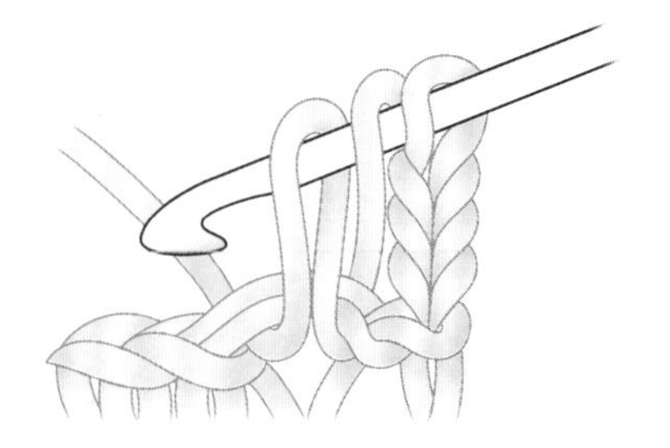

1. Before inserting the hook into the work, wrap the yarn round the hook. Put the hook through the work with the yarn wrapped around, yarn round hook again and pull through the first loop on the hook. You now have 3 loops on the hook.

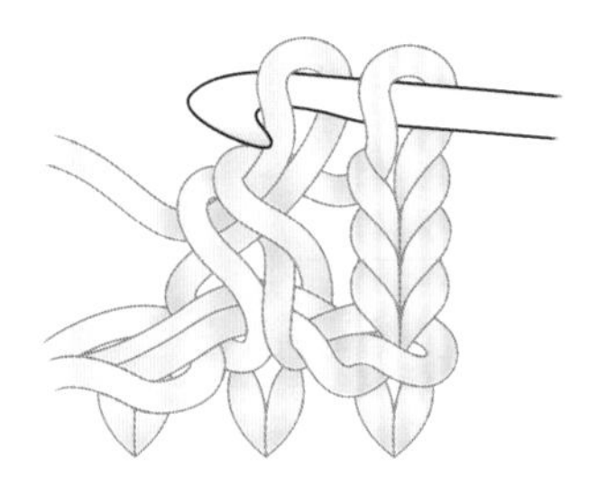

2. Yarn round hook again, pull the yarn through the first 2 loops on the hook. You now have 2 loops on the hook.

3. Pull the yarn through 2 loops again. You will be left with 1 loop on the hook.

Double treble (dtr)

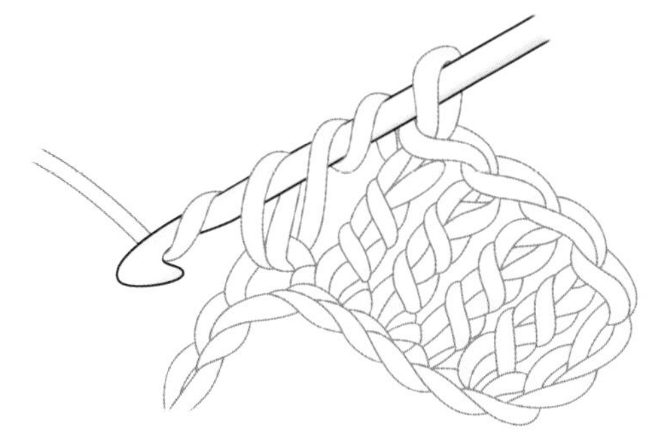

Yarn round hook twice, insert hook into the stitch, yarn round hook, pull a loop through (4 loops on hook), yarn round hook, pull the yarn through 2 stitches (3 loops on hook), yarn round hook, pull a loop through the next 2 stitches (2 loops on hook), yarn round hook, pull a loop through the last 2 stitches.

Front Post treble crochet (FPtr)

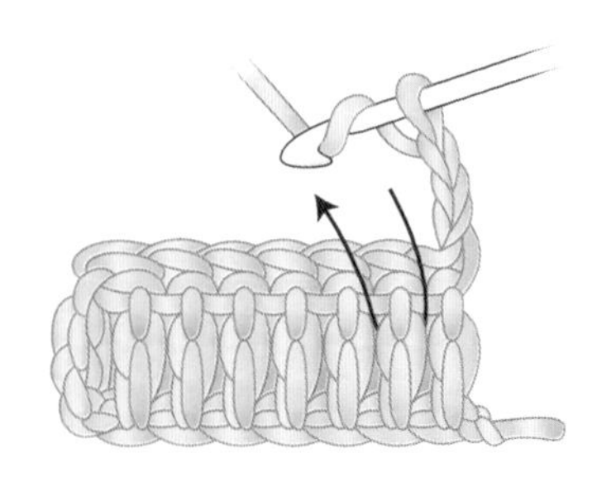

1. Yarn round hook and insert the hook from the front and around the post (the stem) of the next treble crochet from right to left.

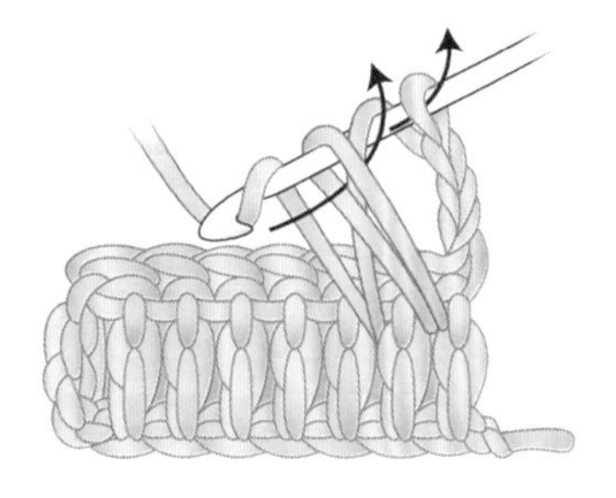

2. Yarn round hook and pull the yarn through the work, yarn round hook and pull the yarn through the first 2 loops on the hook.

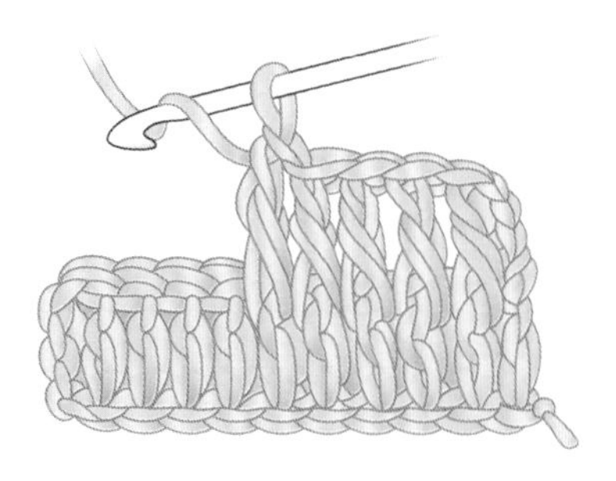

3. Yarn round hook and pull the yarn through the 2 loops on the hook. (1 loop on hook).

One Front Post treble completed.

Increasing

Make two or three stitches into one stitch or space from the previous row. The illustration shows a treble crochet increase being made.

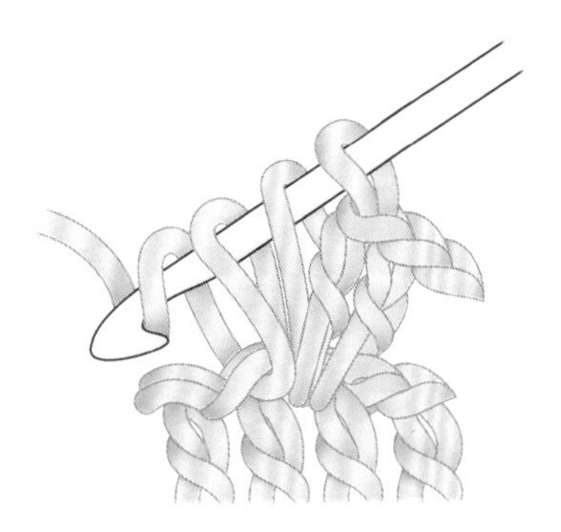

Decreasing

You can decrease by either missing the next stitch and continuing to crochet, or by crocheting two or more stitches together. The basic technique for crocheting stitches together is the same, no matter which stitch you are using. The following examples show dc2tog and tr2tog.

Double crochet two stitches together (dc2tog)

1. Insert the hook into your work, yarn round hook and pull the yarn through the work (2 loops on hook). Insert the hook in next stitch, yarn round hook and pull the yarn through.

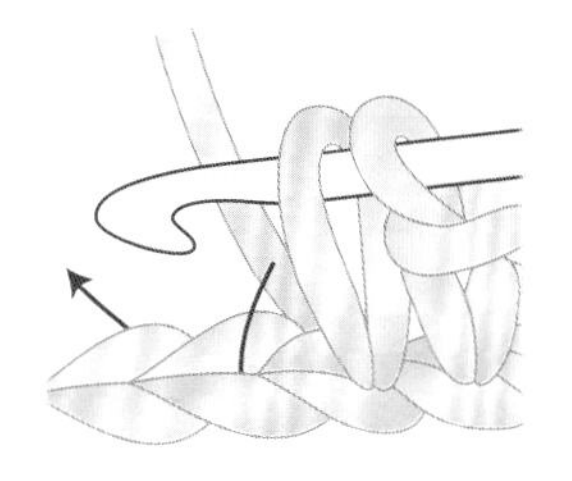

2. Yarn round hook again and pull through all 3 loops on the hook. You will then have 1 loop on the hook.

Treble crochet two stitches together (tr2tog)

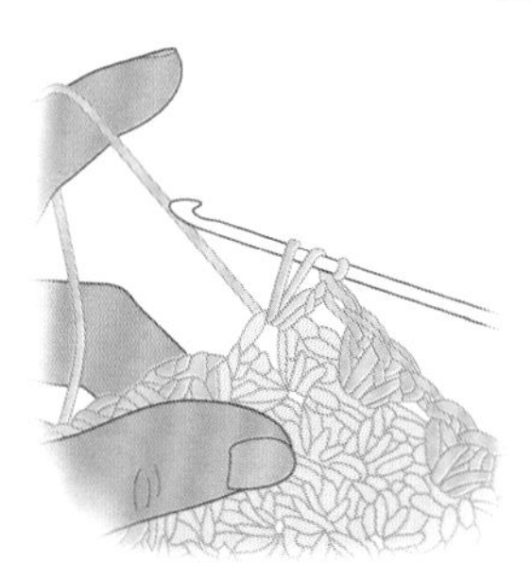

1. Yarn round hook, insert the hook into the next space, yarn round hook, pull the yarn through the work (3 loops on hook).

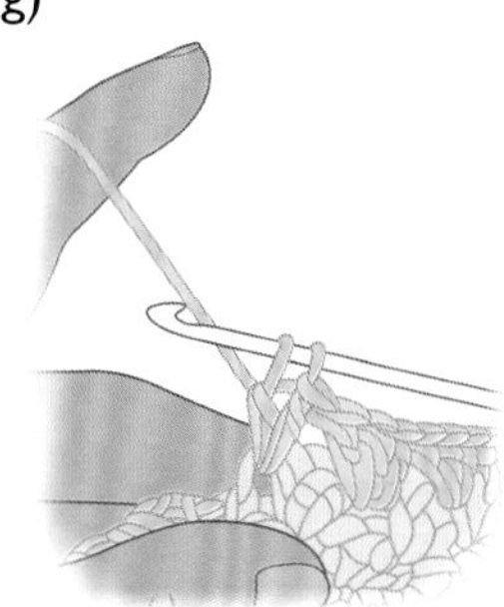

2. Yarn round hook, pull the yarn through 2 loops on the hook (2 loops on hook).

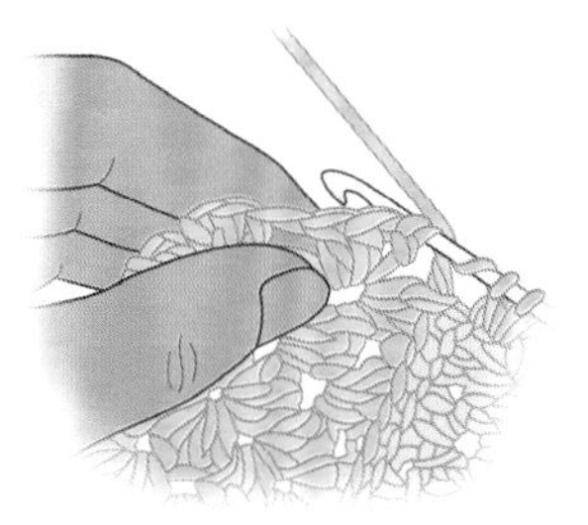

3. Yarn round hook, insert the hook into the next space.

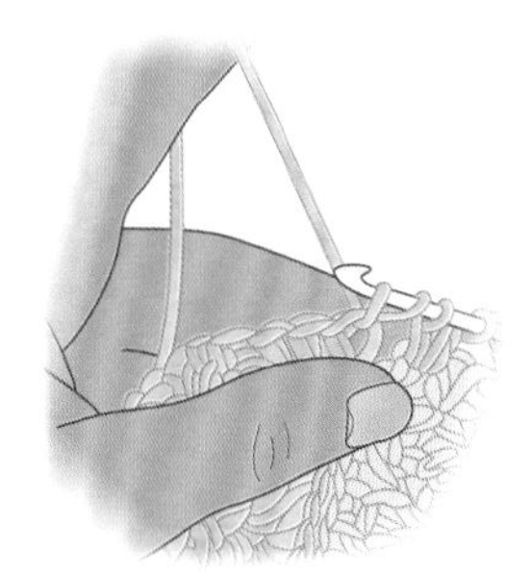

4. Yarn round hook, pull the yarn through the work (4 loops on hook).

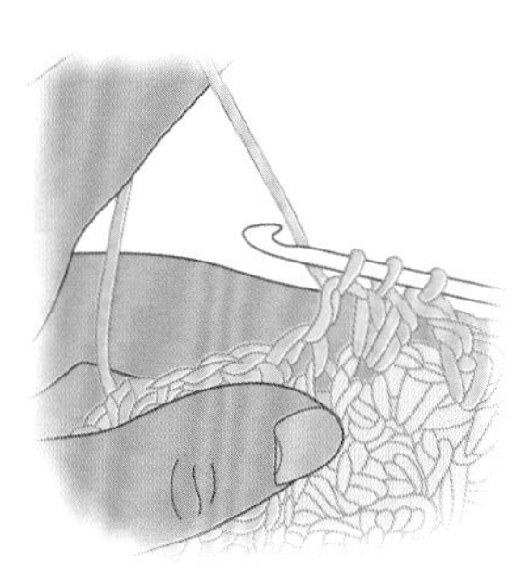

5. Yarn round hook, pull the yarn through 2 loops on the hook (3 loops on hook).

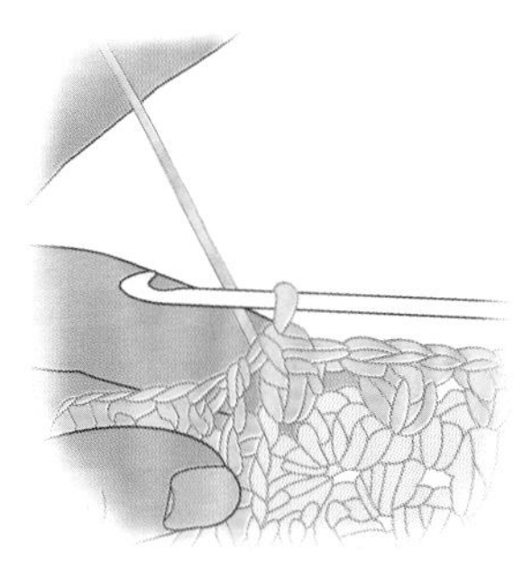

6. Yarn round hook, pull the yarn through all 3 loops on the hook (1 loop on hook). One tr2tog (decrease) made.

Changing colours

Note: You can use this technique when joining in a new ball of yarn as one runs out.

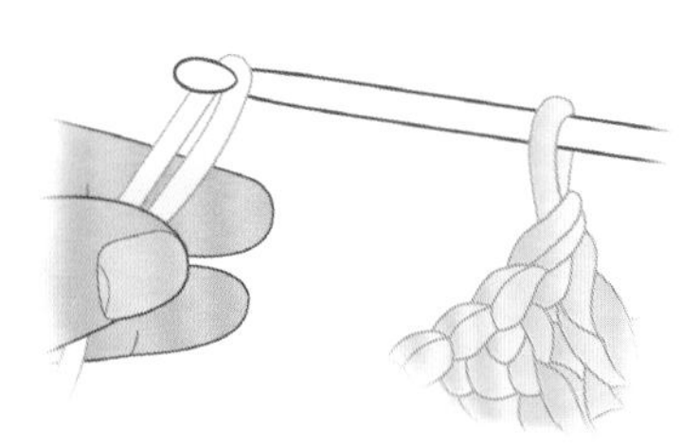

1. Keep the loop of the old yarn on the hook. Drop the tail and catch a loop of the strand of the new yarn with the crochet hook.

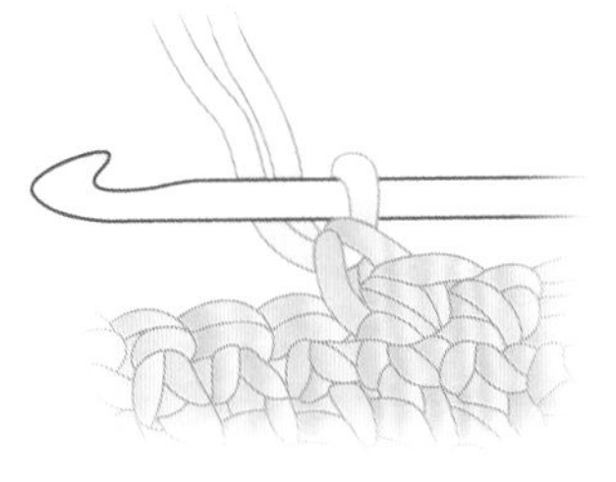

2. Pull the new yarn through the loop on the hook, keeping the old loop drawn tight and continue as instructed in the pattern.

Weaving in yarn ends

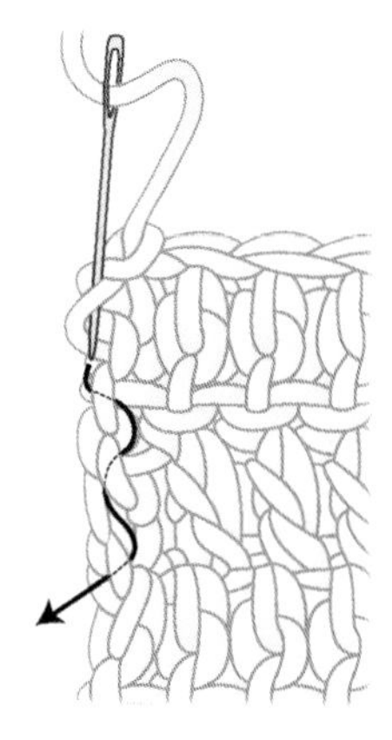

It is important to weave in the tail ends of the yarn so that they are secure and your crochet won't unravel. Thread a tapestry needle with the tail end of yarn. On the wrong side, take the needle through the crochet one stitch down on the edge, then take it through the stitches, working in a gentle zig-zag. Work through four or five stitches then return in the opposite direction. Remove the needle, pull the crochet gently to stretch it, and trim the end.

Sewing up

Sewing up crochet fabric can be done in many ways, but using a whip stitch is the easiest. However, you will be able to see the stitches clearly, so use a matching yarn. Lay the two pieces to be joined next to each other with right sides facing upward. Secure the yarn to one piece. Insert the needle into the front of one piece of fabric, then up from the back of the adjoining fabric. Repeat along the seam.

Blocking

Crochet can tend to curl so to make flat pieces stay flat you may need to block them. Pin the piece out to the correct size and shape on the ironing board, then cover with a cloth and press or steam gently (depending on the type of yarn) and allow to dry completely.

Tassels and fringes

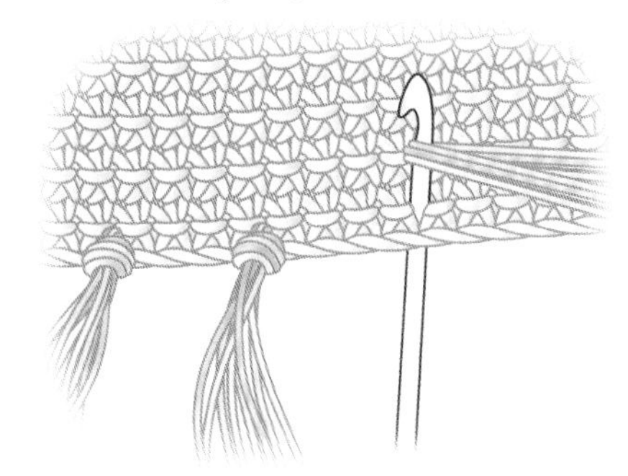

1. Cut yarn to quantity and length given in the pattern. Take suggested number of strands and fold in half. With right side of project facing, insert a crochet hook from the wrong side through one of the edge stitches. Catch the bunch of strands with the hook at the fold point.

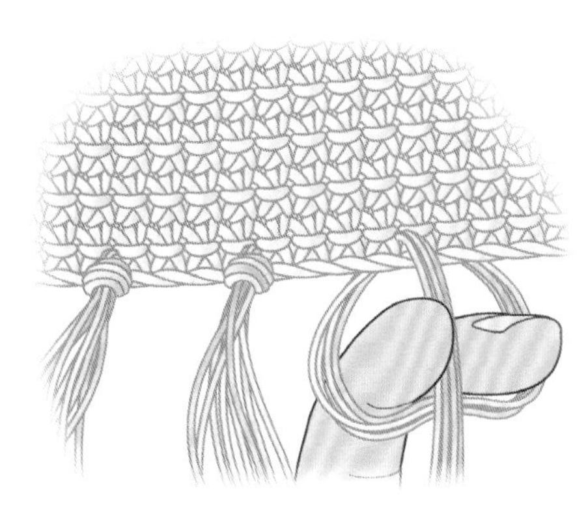

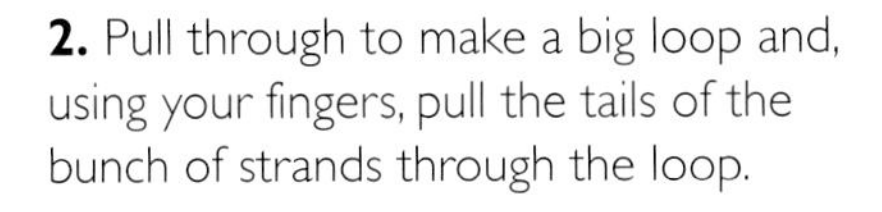

2. Pull through to make a big loop and, using your fingers, pull the tails of the bunch of strands through the loop.

3. Pull on the tails to tighten the loop firmly to secure the tassel.

CROCHET STITCH CONVERSION CHART

Crochet stitches are worked in the same way in both the UK and the USA, but the stitch names are not the same and identical names are used for different stitches. Below is a list of the UK terms used in this book, and the equivalent US terms.

UK TERM	US TERM
double crochet (dc)	single crochet (sc)
half treble (htr)	half double crochet (hdc)
treble (tr)	double crochet (dc)
double treble (dtr)	treble (tr)
triple treble (trtr)	double treble (dtr)
quadruple treble (qtr)	triple treble (trtr)
tension	gauge
yarn round hook (yrh)	yarn over hook (yoh)

SUPPLIERS

Glorious shawls, wraps and cover-ups start with glorious yarns! The shawls in this book have been created using a wide range of different colours, styles and types of yarns, so there is sure to be something you'll love, no matter what your mood or look. Many of them can be made with yarns already stowed away in your stash waiting for that special project, but here is the selection of suppliers used for the wonderful yarns featured.

Artesano

www.artesanoyarns.co.uk

Berroco

www.berroco.com
www.deramores.com

Berisfords Ribbons

www.berisfords-ribbons.co.uk

Buttons & Fastenings

www.minervacrafts.com

Cascade 220

www.cascadeyarns.com
www.deramores.com

Caron

www.deramores.com
www.yarnspirations.com

Debbie Bliss

www.designeryarns.uk.com
www.knittingfever.com
www.deramores.com

Lion Brand

www.lionbrand.com
www.deramores.com

Lily Sugar 'n' Cream

www.deramores.com
www.yarnspirations.com

Louisa Harding

www.knittingfever.com
www.deramores.com
www.designeryarns.uk.com

Malabrigo

www.malabrigoyarn.com
www.deramores.com

Mirasol

www.designeryarns.uk.com
www.deramores.com

Rowan

www.knitrowan.com
www.deramores.com
www.jimmybeanswool.com

Sublime

www.deramores.com
www.sublimeyarns.com

For tools and finishings, the following have store locators on their websites, as well as online sales:

UK

John Lewis: www.johnlewis.com
Hobbycraft: www.hobbycraft.co.uk

USA

Michaels: www.michaels.com
Jo-Ann Fabric and Craft Stores: www.joann.com

INDEX

ACKNOWLEDGMENTS

Creating this book has been an exciting and challenging creative project and it would not have been possible without the help, guidance and support of a number of wonderful people. Thank you to Cindy Richards, Penny Craig, Fahema Khanam and the team at CICO Books who are a joy to work with. Huge thanks to photographers Penny Wincer and Emma Mitchell, and stylist Nel Haynes for the breathtaking photography, also to the editor Rachel Atkinson whose technical wisdom has taught me so much, and to Jemima Bicknell for her meticulous pattern checking!

Thanks also to the companies who supported this book with yarns and materials – Artesano, Cascade Yarns, Deramores, Lion Brand, Rowan, Designer Yarns and Minerva Crafts – your generosity is hugely appreciated.

The last couple of months have seen me crocheting all hours and my friends and families have been nothing short of my own personal cheer squad. Thank you all and I hope that you, and my online friends and readers of www.madepeachy.com enjoy this book as much as I have enjoyed working on it.

Finally, I can probably never express my gratitude enough to my wonderful husband John, who encourages and motivates me every step of the way, and not least, for always reading out the subtitles on movies so I don't have to look up from my crochet!